FBC
5-
8/19

Can a Democrat
get into Heaven?

You
Lovely *to*
see *you* *again* —
Anne

ALSO BY ANNE SHELBY

Poems
Appalachian Studies
Lines From Home

Books for Children
Homeplace
Potluck
We Keep A Store
The Someday House
What To Do About Pollution

Can a
Democrat
get into
Heaven?

POLITICS, RELIGION & OTHER THINGS
YOU AIN'T SUPPOSED TO TALK ABOUT

Columns by

Anne Shelby

with a foreword by
Gurney Norman

Can a Democrat get into Heaven?
by Anne Shelby

ISBN   0-9778745-0-8

Photos by Jamie Johnson
Design by Kate Larken

This first edition published March 2006 by

a division of

PO Box 6034
Louisville, Kentucky 40207
www.Motes.EvaMedia.com

To
Edmund

What're they gonna do?

Contents

Politics

You Scratch My Money, I'll Scratch Yours

Religion

***The Apostle Paul never said anything about
women keeping silent in the newspaper***

Life Gets Teges

Finding the Mundane in the Everyday

Mules, Haints & Asphalt Salesmen

Poor, But We've Got Stories

Occasionally Yours

Muddling Through the Year

They Don't Make 'em Like That Anymore

Memories and Good-byes

≈

Foreword

In the past two decades, Anne Shelby has established herself as one of Kentucky's best and most versatile writers. She is an accomplished poet and writer of books for children. She has written and performed in plays and other theater pieces. She is a popular story-teller, deeply familiar with traditional Appalachian tales. She is also a wonderful singer of the old mountain songs and church hymns.

For the past five years, Anne has also written a personal column for small weekly newspapers in Eastern Kentucky and periodically for *The Lexington Herald-Leader.* Many of her articles are available on-line, giving her a growing audience that numbers in the thousands.

Anne's newspaper subjects are so varied they defy easy summary, but they include politics, religion, women in the Bible, the weather, coal mining and miners, ecological concerns such as mountaintop removal mining, or just the sayings and doings of people in her home community. Anne writes about the old days in Clay and Jackson counties, recounting stories of colorful people from generations back whose words, deeds and antics are still remembered.

Anne lives in the place and among the people she writes about. She was born into the true Eastern Kentucky community of memory and has lived most of her life there. She and her husband Edmund live on Teges Creek in Clay County, in a house built before the Civil

War and where her family has lived for more than a century. Anne's life and art and language are deeply rooted in the local place where she lives. She knows mountain life and people in ways that only a native of the place can know. Her voice is as natural to its native place as a songbird's. Through her writing and other arts she is a memory keeper who addresses the larger world. She is a bearer of local tradition who is at the same time a modern, progressive thinker.

Appearing individually week by week, Anne's newspaper pieces have regularly amused and informed her readers. Now with her articles gathered in the pages of a book, readers have a chance to appreciate Anne's newspaper writing in a fresh way, a literary way. Anne's rare and beautiful language gift has raised the writing of the traditional personal column to an art. First and foremost, Anne is a literary artist, in poetry and prose and in her use of the daily language of mountain people, which in itself is beautiful. Whether she is telling a story or arguing the Bible with certain preachers whose attitudes are hard and unforgiving or satirizing politicians or sharing her own deep feelings about life and love and loss, Anne's writing reveals her great heart, her keen intelligence, and her down-to-earth common sense. This collection is a fine achievement and an enduring one.

— GURNEY NORMAN
Lexington, Kentucky
February 2006

How to Use This Book

I hadn't planned to write an introduction to this book, but I began to feel that the reader deserved some sort of an explanation.

In 1992 my husband and I moved from Lexington, Kentucky, where we had lived for about fifteen years, to my family's old homeplace on Teges Creek in Clay County, in the hills of southeastern Kentucky. I planned to continue writing – at the time I was publishing primarily poetry and children's books – and it was important to me, too, to fit in with people in the local community. Since that community is largely Republican and fundamentalist, I knew that "fitting in" would mean keeping my opinions to myself.

I tried. Honestly I did. But after so long, I just couldn't do it anymore. I started writing a weekly column ("Mouth of Teges") for the local paper, *The Manchester Enterprise.*

I wanted to do this, not just because I was having trouble keeping my mouth shut, but as a way of being a writer in the place where I lived. Mostly, writers work alone; the few people we do work with – agents, editors publishers – aren't anywhere around. We communicate with them and with other writers by mail, telephone or e-mail. I felt in danger of bifurcating, like Wemmick in *Great Expectations*, into my writer self and my Clay County self. Writing a column for the local paper would help me connect my art with the community in which I lived.

Okay, so maybe I didn't think that one through. Maybe writing a liberal column is not the best way to connect with a conservative community. But, again, there was the whole not-being-able-to-keep-my-mouth-shut-anymore thing.

The pages of *The Manchester Enterprise*, like those of many small weeklies, are filled with local columnists, of which there are three major types: (1) preachers, (2) "society" columnists, and (3) crackpots. There is some overlap. I proudly placed myself in the "crackpot" category and wrote on a variety of topics: local stories, everyday life, religion, politics, holidays and anything else I could think of under deadline. As a lover of language and as a native of southeastern Kentucky, I sometimes claimed the right to write in a traditional Appalachian voice.

Some of these columns were written during a time in which I had affiliated myself with a local church. This was a good and important experience, though ultimately my views and those of the church diverged too much for me to stay.

Other columns I wrote in response to assertions by male fundamentalist preacher columnists, of which *The Manchester Enterprise* had, it seemed to me, a disproportionate number. I didn't think they should get to have the newspaper all to themselves – not all the time, anyway. I wanted my columns to reflect views which would probably not appear in the paper otherwise, but which I suspected might be shared by others in the community, who were better at keeping their mouths shut.

As it turns out, I was right about that. In letters, phone calls, e-mails, and whispered remarks at the doctor's office, gas station and grocery store, people told me they agreed with me – about women's roles, about corruption in the local political system, about George Bush, the war in Iraq, gay civil rights, hillbilly plays, and mountaintop removal mining. But they were afraid to say these things out loud.

One column, "A Woman's Place," challenges the traditional practice of limiting women's work in the church to the nursery, the choir, and the Sunday School class. The week that column appeared, I came home one day to find a message on my telephone answering machine from an older woman who did not leave her name: "That article you wrote – " she said, in a raspy, barely audible voice, "honey, that was ever word the truth."

I was surprised at the number of women who told me that all their lives they had felt the call to preach but knew their church would not permit it.

"Regime Change" and "Lonely Life of a Clay County Democrat" brought local Democrats out of the closet and the woodwork. Some said they were registered Republican, but their hearts belonged to the Democrats.

A checkout clerk told me that when she and her husband get the paper every week, they turn to my column first. "What's she saying now?" the husband always asks.

But of course not all the responses have been positive. Sometimes family and friends have worried that I might be shot or otherwise inconvenienced by someone with strong views in other directions. But nothing like that has happened. I mean really, what're they gonna do?

What they have done – and appropriately so – is write back. In "Breakin' Up Winter," I described a trip to Lexington during which I bought a somewhat "flamboyant" new outfit. The following week, a fellow columnist responded under the heading "Godly Women Should Dress Modestly."

My concern about the increasingly unholy alliance between church and state in this country ("Thou Shalt Not Display the Ten Commandments at the Courthouse") elicited a response from another columnist under a 40 pt. screaming headline: "Somebody is Wrong, Wrong, Wrong!"

But the column which stirred up the biggest

hornet's nest was "The Gays, the Bishops and the Robinsons," written the week after Kentucky native Gene Robinson became the first openly gay Episcopal bishop. Responses to that column included one mean-spirited and largely incoherent letter to the editor which appeared under the heading, "Shelby, Get Right with God."

The flap wasn't so much about my approval of gays as church leaders (though this was a point of some concern) as that I seemed to be making fun of local preachers. And I guess I was. But making fun of preachers, telling preacher stories and preacher jokes, is a time-honored tradition in Kentucky. Appalachian scholar Loyal Jones has collected a whole book of them. Such stories mitigate some of the seriousness and reverence surrounding preachers, acknowledge their humanity, and let some air in around the choke-hold they maintain on the culture.

But the times they are a-changing, and not necessarily for the better. Criticizing authority figures, from the President to the local preacher, has become something of a radical thing to do.

After writing several years for *The Manchester Enterprise* and, later, *The Beattyville Enterprise*, I wanted to offer the column to other small papers in eastern Kentucky, with the aim of adding to the diversity of opinions expressed in those papers also. The Kentucky Foundation for Women supported that goal and in 2005 awarded me a one-year grant to help with the work. That same year, I wrote a regular column for *The Lexington Herald-Leader;* some of those columns are also included in this collection.

I thank the Kentucky Foundation for Women for its support, and I thank my friends and colleagues at *The Manchester Enterprise, The Beattyville Enterprise, The Jackson Times, The Lexington Herald-Leader,* and other papers throughout Kentucky that have published these columns.

I am indebted to various people for stories, ideas,

quotes and information, and I have tried to acknowledge these, where appropriate, in the text.

I thank Lynne and Bettie for their proofreading, Graham and Gabrielle for their unflagging enthusiasm, Sharon for the imaging miracle, Nyoka for good advice, and Kate for her patience, generosity and general competence.

How to use this book? Well, you could use it as a door stopper, window propper, or table leg replacer. I hope you might also find it useful to cheer, encourage and warm you in these rather chilling times.

– ANNE SHELBY
Teges, Kentucky
February 2006

Politics

YOU SCRATCH MY MONEY,
I'LL SCRATCH YOURS

Long Hot Dry Weird Summer

In the spring, the creek behind the house over-flowed its banks, leaving behind a morning-after landscape strewn with plastic, Styrofoam, and beer cans. By midsummer, the flood had diminished to a trickle. Then the creek stopped flowing altogether.

For a time after that, water still stood in the deeper places in the creek bed. The dogs found them and plopped down on their bellies, smiling and panting. Those pools have dried up now, and the rocks in the creek are covered with dark leaves.

❧

"I can't write," I complained, to everybody within earshot. "I'm dried up, like the creek. Everything's weird."

"Write about that," they suggested, rather more cheerfully, I thought, than the situation warranted.

❧

The calendar says 2005, and this must be right because I cannot operate my computer, camera, telephone or TV. In some ways I feel teleported into a future in which I am awkward and old-fashioned, in which everything I know and believe has become obsolete.

In other ways, none of them good, we seem to be moving backwards in time. Sometimes it feels like 1925 again, and we are in Dayton, Tennessee, with Clarence Darrow and William Jennings Bryan, arguing about evolution.

❧

In another flashback, I find myself singing "Black Waters," Jean Ritchie's 1967 song about strip mining. It's a good song, which by now should have found an honored place in retrospectives on protest movements and the Great Folk Scare.

Instead, mountaintop removal and the recent spate of mine spills in Eastern Kentucky have made the song timely again. "Sad scenes of destruction on every hand. Black waters, black waters run down through the land."

❧

My first tobacco buyout check came last week.

"Tobacco's over with," a neighbor told me earlier in the summer, as we pitched dusty tobacco sticks from my barn into the bed of his pickup. He wanted them for "sticking" beans and peas in his garden.

Until this summer my family grew tobacco for as many summers as I can remember. It's strange, I know, waxing sentimental about carcinogens, but there are things I will miss – white canvas on the plant beds, the growing leaves, the pink blossoms, the cut tobacco like tepees in the field, the smell of it in the barn, the tobacco check that always came just in time for Christmas.

And I'll miss the rowdy crews of neighbors rolling in to help set, cut, hang or strip. These activities bound us together and, early spring to late fall, set the rhythm for our lives.

❧

As the weather, the war in Iraq, and the protest against it heated up, a Clay County man was shot and killed by a friend of his at a flea market in Floyd County. They had been arguing about the war.

≈

Though I'm no fan of Kentucky Governor Ernie Fletcher, I take no delight in the summer's reports of scandal in Frankfort. Some people claim that the Democrats have caused more scandals than the Republicans, so the Republicans are entitled to this one. But Republicans have as many scandals as Democrats. It's just that theirs are less interesting and therefore less memorable.

Democratic scandals usually have to do with sex, while Republican scandals are generally about money and regulations, and are therefore harder to follow and understand, and far less stimulating to the imagination.

≈

Despite the long, dry spell and the summer's weirdness, I remain hopeful, searching the horizon for signs of rain and sanity. Politics, I remind myself, is like Kentucky weather, and you know what they say about that.

Stick around. It'll change.

8/22/05

Lonely Life of
a Clay County Democrat

"A *strong Democrat,"* people say, as if they were describing an onion, or something else with a decidedly pungent odor.

Or they'll call you "a b-a-a-a-a-d Democrat," which puts you in the same category as a bad outlaw or a bad case of the flu.

Some people even say there aren't any Democrats in Clay County, but there are. Most of them are living in caves up on Redbird, where they've been hiding out since 1898, when Tom Baker got shot and lost the Baker-White feud.

And the rest of us, we're sort of a pitiful bunch, hunkered over and squirrelly-acting, beat down and beat back till we're afraid to speak above a whisper. When we do, it's to mutter idealistic, out-of-date phrases nobody wants to hear anymore, something about providing health care, saving the planet, and standing up for the little guy.

This county is so heavily Republican, when you go to the county clerk's office to register to vote, they just assume you're going to register Republican. If you say, no, Democrat, they act a little annoyed. They have to scrounge around to find another form and dust it off.

I certainly do not mean to imply that anyone ever elected to the office of county clerk in Clay – or in neighboring Jackson County, for that matter – would do anything that was the least bit questionable. But a lot of people have told me they registered Republican when they went in there aiming to register Democrat.

Everybody says, "If you register Democrat you can't vote in the primary." Which is a lie. Of course you can vote in the primary. You just can't vote in the Republican part of the primary.

When they say, "You can't vote in the primary," what they really mean is, "You might as well not vote in the primary. Because everybody knows no Democratic candidate has a snowball's chance of winning in the general election. And what's more, this will never change. So forget about it here's your Republican registration form T-shirt and bumper sticker good-bye."

In other words, we've got a one-party system.

Not only do they assume everybody's going to register Republican, they also assume everybody's going to vote the straight Republican ticket.

I was working as an election officer in the last Presidential election when an older woman, a registered Republican, came in to vote. She said she couldn't see well and asked for help. One of the Republican judges went in the voting booth with her, but only bothered to point out one candidate. "Right here is George Bush's name," she said helpfully.

"Well, I don't want to vote for HIM!" the old woman squalled.

If you're a Democrat in Clay County, people question, not just your politics, but your religion, too. I have actually heard more than one debate, by people who were not trying to be funny, about whether or not a Democrat could get into heaven.

Now I don't believe political party affiliation is going to be one of the criteria for passing through the pearly gates. I believe we'll see all political parties represented in that bright city.

And Clay County Democrats, who have suffered so much in this life, will surely have a special place.

11/14/02

Praise the Lord – and the FBI

*T**he ongoing federal investigation*** of drug trafficking and political corruption in Clay County is cause for celebration here.

Clay Countians are far from stupid, and hardly naïve. We have known all along about the corruption in our local political system.

We have known about the vote buying, the cronyism, the nepotism, the sweet deals political officials arrange for themselves, and about their general disregard for the public good. We have suspected some local officials of being in cahoots with drug dealers, and recent revelations seem to bear out those suspicions.

Some dealers appear to operate with impunity. Others are said to receive convenient and timely warnings when a bust is imminent.

We have never gotten used to this kind of corruption, but we have lived with it for so long that we have come to expect it and to believe there is nothing we can do about it.

We heard our parents, grandparents, and great-grandparents say the same things, and we repeated them: "There's no law in Clay County." "Better not stir up a hornet's nest." "Politics is a dirty business. Good people stay out of it."

This kind of resignation came, not so much out of the cultural fatalism sometimes attributed to Appalachia, but out of a not unrealistic fear of going up against the local power structure, the people with the money, the jobs, and the influence over almost everything in the county. In such a lopsided contest, all one seemed likely to win was a night in jail or the emergency room, or perhaps star billing at the funeral home. At best, one would be insuring that no one in his or her family would ever get a job in the county again.

We have watched in helpless horror as old patterns persisted and our county became awash in drugs.

But the times they are a-changing. New leaders are emerging to operate outside the good-old-boy network. A "court watch" group has organized. About a third of the county's citizens turned out for a march against drugs. Citizens' groups are working to bring better drug treatment facilities here. Local churches are providing counseling for addicts and their families. Every week the local paper, *The Manchester Enterprise*, reports drug busts, large and small.

And a federal investigation has broken up a major interstate drug ring headquartered in Manchester, involving a former county clerk, an election officer and other public servants. The best news is that the investigation is continuing. We have yet to touch bottom there.

And we are unlikely to forget soon, though they have understandably kept a low profile of late, that the defense attorneys in that case included our local state senator and the president of the Kentucky Senate, who ought to have shown, if not better character, at least better judgment and better sense.

Some attribute recent dramatic changes to the power of prayer, others to the tenacity of investigators.

It is encouraging to see the strength and energy of local churches being brought to bear on the county's problems. And given the strength of the local politicians' grip on the county's throat, it is easy to understand the belief that nothing short of Divine Intervention could help.

But we also need to credit the FBI, and the people who put themselves in danger to gather evidence. Whether it was the Lord, the FBI, or both, Clay County has a chance now to become something other than one of the state's primary examples of political corruption and persistent poverty.

But I worry that not even heaven and the FBI can change Clay County. I worry that even if we get rid of all the old crooks, we will turn around and vote in new ones, because "good people stay out of politics" and because in Clay County, as elsewhere, power is never given up easily.

That is my fear. My hope is that honest and competent candidates will think they have a chance, finally, in Clay County politics, and will run for office in next year's elections and win. That will take work and commitment on the part of Clay Countians, and continued monitoring from outside.

My fellow *Manchester Enterprise* columnist Myrtle Shoupe says, Let's all continue to pray. And I would add, let's keep those FBI, Attorney General, and drug tip hotline numbers handy.

11/17/05

Welcome to Coal Country

***P**eople from other states* might not think so, but it is possible to grow up in Kentucky and still know almost nothing about horses. It is even possible to grow up in Eastern Kentucky and still know almost nothing about coal.

When I was a girl we lived in Jackson County, where my dad was from. As a teenager I lived in Laurel County. Weekends, summers and holidays we spent in Clay County, where my mother's family lived.

The hills in these counties, along the western edge of the Appalachian mountain range, are lower and softer than the mountains further east. But there is coal and mining in these counties, too, and was when I was growing up there in the 1950s and '60s.

I sang along with Tennessee Ernie Ford when "Sixteen Tons" made the Hit Parade, but I knew nothing about coal mining, had little connection with it, and did not think about it, one way or another.

The people I knew taught school, kept store, grew tobacco or raised cattle. They worked at factories in Ohio and drove home on the weekends. I did not know any coal miners.

The world of coal and mining existed in the same space and time as my world, but like energy escaping from another dimension, it intersected with my world only in odd moments.

We had electric heat at our house, so the coal that

warmed us was far away, and we did not see it. But at my grandparents' houses, the connection between coal and heat was immediate and direct.

The coal pile in the yard began life as a small peaked mountain in the fall, and shrank and flattened through the winter as it was hauled into the house, bucket by bucket, and dumped in the grate to burn.

The coal was a dead weight when I carried it in the heavy bucket, fingers curled painfully around the metal handle. But the magic of fire brought the coal back to life, and it hissed and popped, whistled and cracked, setting flames to leaping up the chimney and shadows to dancing wildly on the ceiling and the walls.

About three miles from my grandparents' house there was an underground mine. Sometimes miners came to my grandparents' store on their break, their faces still covered with coal dust. There might be a cut-up in the bunch, who laughed too loud and liked to prank, but mostly the men sat or stood quietly around the store, eating crackers and Vienna sausages, drinking Pepsi and smoking cigarettes till it was time to jump in the back of somebody's pickup and head back to the mine.

My grandmother usually kept the store, but my grandfather took over when the miners came. Ma said it smothered her to think about the men working in a low tight place back under the hill.

Before the Daniel Boone Parkway, to get from Laurel to Clay County, we took 80 East, which curved up, down and around a series of mountains, offering both scenic views and, for those of us inclined to carsickness, several good chances to throw up.

At Horse Creek, just outside Manchester, trees, gardens, flowers, even weeds seemed to vanish. Mowed fields and wooded hills gave way to tipples and railroad cars. Tracks cut across the road and ran alongside it. Houses crouched close together in sad colorless rows.

It did not occur to me then to wonder why the only place in the whole area that had any industry was the poorest looking place of all.

It is possible to grow up in Kentucky and not know about coal. It is possible to go to school, live, and work in Kentucky and not know about coal. It is not possible to live in Kentucky and not be affected by coal.

It isn't just that the mining of coal alters the landscape and poisons the water supply. It isn't just that the transporting of coal tears up the roads, or that the burning of coal pollutes the air. Coal money finances the campaigns of politicians on the local, state and national levels. It helps determine who makes the decisions in our state, and whom those decisions benefit.

Maybe you never saw a miner in your life. The bulldozers never came near your house. A boulder never crashed down the mountain into your bedroom. You never woke to find your yard covered in black goo from a sludge pond spill.

Your grandfather did not die of black lung, your father in a roof fall, your brother in a mine explosion. Your cousin did not lose a leg in the mines, your brother-in-law a hand. Your buddy from high school did not die in a head-on collision with an overloaded coal truck.

Still, even if you don't know a coal mine from a hole in the ground, a strip job from burlesque, if you're in Kentucky, welcome to coal country.

10/27/05

Run Over Bad Bill
With Overloaded Gravel Truck

Okay, now I'm mad. Before this, I was just depressed, disillusioned, baffled, stunned, incredulous, somewhat annoyed, and hovering hopelessly on the brink of despair. But now I'm mad.

For nearly twenty years, coal trucks in Kentucky have enjoyed an exemption from the legal 40-ton weight limit. Now, in its wisdom, the state house of representatives has voted, not, as one might hope, to do away with this nutty exemption, but to let other trucks haul loads over the legal limit, too.

If the bill passes the Senate, we'll soon have, along with the coal trucks barreling down the highways, trucks hauling sixty tons of sand, gravel, gas or oil.

I don't know about where you live, but around here it's already Demolition Derby, what with narrow roads, curves, hills, coal trucks, log trucks, rolling meth labs, and drivers under the influence of everything from alcohol to Xanax.

Let's see a show of hands. How many have ever come face to face with Grim Death in the form of an overloaded coal truck coming at you at high speed, and well over on your side of the road?

From here it looks like a sea of hands going up in Eastern Kentucky.

If this ever happens to you, you remember it. You remember where you were, the grill of the truck close

36

up, how grateful you were for that little bit of shoulder to pull off on, and how you had to sit there awhile even after the danger passed, trying to remember how to breathe.

Out for a Sunday drive in the Triumph with the top down, thirty-some years ago, I held the baby in my lap while my husband drove. We were on old 25-E between Corbin and Barbourville when the truck came at us – fast and in our lane.

Edmund pulled the wheel hard to the right, and we landed on a narrow strip of ground between the highway and the railroad track. The truck went on. It hadn't hit us. It had just run us off the road, shaken us up, and provided us with a recurring image for anxiety attacks and nightmares. We got off easy that time.

Last Labor Day we packed a cooler and a picnic basket and headed for Buckhorn Lake, where we planned to laze away the afternoon on a grassy bank, observing the habits of trees.

We had not planned on the near-death experience, but on the narrow road that winds up Bullskin Creek from Clay into Leslie County, we met an enormous truck careening downhill on the wrong side of the road, seemingly out of control.

We were lucky that time, too, but not everybody is. Too many weeks, the local paper runs a "fatal car crash" story, with a color picture on the front page of an overturned vehicle, the pavement around it strewn with shattered glass and twisted metal. On an inside page, the family thanks all those who sent food and flowers, and runs a picture of their "lost loved one." Every year on the anniversary of the death, they run the picture again – a young man in a prom tuxedo, a middle-aged woman, or a pretty girl with a dated hairdo, trapped for all time in grainy black and white.

House Bill 8 would dramatically increase highway fatalities in Kentucky, some legislators argued, and would cost the state millions in added road repairs. So if this bill is so bad, why was it even proposed? And why did it pass the House?

Did I miss something? Was there a public outcry for expanded weight limits on trucks? Was there a story on the news about Kentuckians marching on Frankfort or overwhelming lawmakers with e-mails demanding more heavy trucks on the roads?

No, because we won't any of us benefit from this bill. So who would?

The coal industry will benefit, since the bill heads off any court challenge to coal's present cozy arrangement with the law. And the change would be a bonanza for construction companies, who could make money tearing up the roads running overloaded trucks, and then by getting state contracts to repair them. And the politicians who accept big contributions from these companies, they would benefit, too.

But we're not talking about economics here, and we're not talking about the survival of the coal industry, which has been threatening to pull out of the state ever since they came in and dug the first hole.

No, friends, we're talking politics: good old-fashioned, down-and-dirty, wheeling-and-dealing, smoked-filled-back-room, crooked-as-a-dog's-hind-leg, you-scratch-my-money-and-I'll-scratch-yours Kentucky politics.

2/24/05

I Have Been to the Mountaintop –
But It Wasn't There

*I*magine a sun-filled afternoon in spring, the hillsides leafing into a thousand shades of green, rain water rushing over creek rocks, the air alive with the call of songbirds, the flutter of wings.

Now imagine a flat barren place, drained of color, void of sound, where nothing grows but spindly grass, in ground reduced to sun-baked clay, littered with shale and sandstone. Not even an insect stirs.

Is this a description of (a) heaven and hell, (b) the mountains and the desert, (c) the past and the future, or (d) Eastern Kentucky, before and after mountaintop removal coal mining?

The correct answer: all of the above, but give yourself extra points if you picked (d).

Recently I traveled to Leslie and Perry counties with a group of Kentucky authors to look at mountain-top removal. Like me, many of the writers were from Eastern Kentucky. Some of us live in coal counties, on land that has been in our families for generations.

It seems that while we have not been paying attention, while we were busy or thinking about something else, the coal trucks have hauled a lot of Eastern Kentucky away. What they have left doesn't even look like Eastern Kentucky anymore, but more like a dead planet.

This wasn't supposed to happen. Regulations

passed in the 1970s were intended to limit damage from surface mining, not make it worse. But giant earth-moving machines, some twenty stories high, have been roaring through a loophole in the law ever since.

Mountaintops can be taken off and not replaced, the law says, only where the land is to be put to some "better use," like commercial, residential, or recreational development. But except for a few showplaces, the land is not being put to better use, and most likely never will be.

In remote areas, without water or trees, where even the skyline has been altered, it's hard to imagine anyone ever wanting even to go to these places, let alone live, shop or play there. We toured both working sites and abandoned ones, and the old sites didn't look much better than the new.

Until recently, most mountaintop removal sites tended to be off the beaten path. To get there, you had to turn off the main road, onto gravel and then dirt, then take some kind of ATV, but finally you had to get out and walk. Now, so much mining has been done, many sites are visible from the road.

Still, from the ground, you can see only a little of what's going on. To really see, you have to go up in the air.

At the Hazard airport, we took turns climbing into two small planes, four-seaters, for a ride over Perry County. What I saw then has saddened me beyond the telling of it. Everywhere, in every direction, the earth has been laid bare, stripped of vegetation, the creeks and precious topsoil buried under tons of rock and clay.

"How typical is this?" I asked the pilot, hollering above the noise of the engine.

"It's like this all the way to Virginia," she said.

State and federal enforcement agencies have, for the most part, stood by and watched as mountaintop removal, which was supposed to be the exception, has become the rule. In administrations interested in cheap energy and high profits, even the lax laws we have now are not always enforced.

For future generations, mountaintop removal will have destroyed their water supply and turned tillable ground into wasteland. But we don't have to look into the future to see the damage. Mountaintop removal is hurting Eastern Kentuckians right now.

Yes, it provides jobs, but mountaintop removal provides far fewer jobs than other forms of mining, because it replaces miners with machines. More responsible mining methods, a diversified economy, and the development of alternative energy sources would add jobs, not take jobs away.

On our tour, folks from around Eastern Kentucky told us what it's like to live with mountaintop removal. The nearly constant blasting can drive you crazy, give your kids nightmares, tear up your well, poison your water, and crack the foundation of your house.

Speeding overloaded coal trucks add to the noise pollution and endanger lives. Creeks filled with sediment overflow their banks, flooding roads, houses and fields. And the dust settles on everything, including you, if you're brave enough to step outside.

When I got back to my own mountain home, I couldn't help but imagine those giant machines tearing into these familiar hillsides, where my grandparents and great-grandparents grew corn, where I played as a child, where now I go for walks and to talk with God. And I almost could not stand the thoughts of it. For mountain people, to destroy our hills is to destroy us, too.

Nobody is saying that coal should not be mined. We are saying that coal should be mined in such a way that it doesn't destroy our land, our water, and our lives in the process.

5/05/05

41

Parkway to Prayer

Well me and Edmund went over to London a-Saturday to visit with my sister Jessie Lynne that lives over there she is having a birthday this week. Happy Birthday Sis! HA HA

We didn't go on the old Daniel Boone Parkway we went on the new HAL ROGERS PARKWAY.

Hit seemed like hit was about as bumpy from coal trucks and log trucks and about as dangerous and took about the same amount of time as the old Daniel Boone Parkway. There wasn't no toll booths on it but I swear I'd ruther pay a toll ever time as to have to call it the HAL ROGERS PARKWAY.

Hit just don't sound right, like changing the name of the First Church of God to Joe's Bar and Grill.

Some say Daniel Boone weren't nothing but a man that left his family to go off and claim the best land for the rich people and leave the rest of it for us. And I reckon if Ol' Dan'l hadn't of found the Cumberland Gap and pointed the way west, somebody else would have probly figured it out sooner or later. We wouldn't be all still backed up along the coast, crowded up, no elbow room, wondering which direction to go.

But whatever Ol' Dan'l's shortcomings in real life, in our minds he is bigger than life. He is a myth, he is a legend, he was a man, a big man, from the coonskin cap on top of Ol' Dan to the heels of his rawhide shoes. Daniel Boone is a symbol of courage, independence, and closeness to nature, whereas HAL ROGERS is, well, a Republican from Somerset.

I hope this is not the start of a trend. I don't want to live in the HAL ROGERS National Forest nor ride the HAL ROGERS Transit Bus nor view a outdoor drama named THE LEGEND OF HAL ROGERS.

I don't mean to throw off on HAL ROGERS but if they was bound and determined to name something HAL ROGERS I wish they'd a named something HAL ROGERS that didn't already have a perfectly good name and something that was maybe a little bit closer to Somerset.

Now that's just the way I feel about it and you can call it the HAL ROGERS PARKWAY if you want to but I've been calling it the Daniel Boone for thirty years and don't aim to change now they can put up all the signs they want to.

In other news, Christians are being asked to pray and I go along with that. Let's all pray that the Lord will move and give us a new President.

7/20/03

Hard to Swaller

We have all known for some time about the dangers that lurk in the grocery store. The insecticides in the produce, the fat in the meats, the cholesterol in the dairy products, the chemicals and preservatives in the processed foods. What we did not know till now was how dangerous it is to eat a pretzel.

I heard on the news that the President of the United States was just sitting on the couch in the White House this past Sunday watching a football game on TV, and Laura was in the other room. It didn't say what she was doing. I guess she's not a big football fan. Anyway, about 5:30 in the evening the President reached and got him a pretzel and put it in his mouth and it didn't go down right some way or another and he passed out and fell on the floor and hit his face.

When George the Elder was the President and went to Japan on a state visit, he ended up vomiting under the table. Which is not considered good manners in Japan.

Anyway, they said what happened to George the Younger was, not that he choked or smothered or anything, because that would not be Presidential. They said that the pretzel hit a nerve in his neck, and that caused his heart to slow down, and that caused him to pass out.

Well, I know it sounds peculiar and of course we never have heard of anything remotely like this ever happening before, but if that's what they said then it must be the truth, or they wouldn't say it, would they?

If they say that the President of the United States passed out from eating a pretzel, then we as Americans have no business questioning that. We cannot have people going around questioning things, especially when we are at war. Besides, we're tired of questioning things. We don't want to question things any more, and we don't want to hear anybody else questioning things, either.

So if they say he passed out from a pretzel, we have to believe it. If they say it's a good idea to give rich people back the money they paid in taxes, then we have to believe it. If they say it's all right to throw out the laws we've made to try to keep our air clean enough to breathe and our water clean enough to drink, then I guess we'll have to go along with it. If they say we have to keep right on and on dropping bombs on a poor country where a lot of people are already starving and driven from their homes, then I guess we have to believe that, too.

It's just that some things, like that durn pretzel, are a little bit hard to swaller.

1/17/02

Regime Change

I **walked into** a restaurant in Manchester the other morning, set down and ordered a cup of coffee. At a table on the other side of the room, some fellers were talking about the world situation. Which, as we all know, is not that good.

I'd missed the first part of the conversation, but I heard the rest of it. I listen to the news, so I caught on to who they were talking about.

There has to be a regime change, one feller was saying, because this particular leader has got weapons of mass destruction. At the very least he could cost us thousands of American lives. At the worst he could trigger World War III.

And he can't be trusted, another feller said, because of the way he sees things. He believes the Almighty is all on HIS side. He believes his enemies are the enemies of God and servants of the Great Satan. The way they talked, this leader makes his decisions, not based on facts, but on ambition, fear, hatred and revenge.

And all the time he's been getting ready for war, they said, his country's needed schools and hospitals and jobs. It's the old people, children, the sick and the poor that suffer most.

They talked like this leader had isolated himself from other nations, backed out of treaties his own coun- try had already signed, and ignored the United Nations.

It sounded like he had got the people in his own country to where they were either brainwashed into going along with everything he said, or afraid to speak out against him. He hadn't been elected, they said, but had come to power by dubious means, and ever since then he'd been working to gain even more power for himself.

One feller allowed that the whole thing was really about oil. This leader came out of a family that had got rich off oil, he said. He knows the wealth and the power of oil, and if he wants it, he'll take it.

Like I say, I didn't hear the start of the conversation. But from what I heard I had to go along with it. This leader sounded dangerous, and certainly not like somebody you'd want running a country.

Then they said that to get rid of him, we ought to drop a big lot of bombs around on different places where he stays at. But I had to disagree with them there, dropping bombs on Crawford, Texas, Washington, D.C., and Kennebunkport, Maine. It won't do. A lot of innocent people would get hurt and killed.

No, I say let's just get rid of this leader the regular way, by voting him out of office next election.

10/17/02

State of the Onion

I didn't listen to the President's State of the Union speech. It's not that I wasn't interested. But I didn't want to be distracted by the TV-show aspects of it. And I didn't want the news people telling me what I ought to think. So I printed it off the Internet and studied it myself – what it said and what it didn't say.

There was only one sentence about education. Bush claimed to have achieved "historic education reform." He did not mention that he had actually cut funds to education, and that his "reform" is mostly just requiring schools do more testing. Some people think they're testing too much already.

Recent corporate scandals, stock market declines, growing deficits and job losses were hardly mentioned, and the President did not explain how we are going to pay for things like Project Bio-Shield, AIDS relief in Africa and a war in Iraq while still cutting taxes, mostly on the rich.

Things like the economy, job creation, health insurance and prescription drug coverage, the President wants to stay out of, leaving them mostly to the business world to fix. He did not explain why this will work now when it never did before.

Most of the speech was about Iraq. I don't remember Bush saying anything about taking on Iraq when he was running for President. He didn't even start talking about it till after September 11. Since then, he's been trying to get us to identify Iraq with terrorism. The State of the Union speech seemed designed to make us wad our fears, our anger and our patriotism into one big ball and aim it at Iraq.

"Imagine those 19 hijackers with other weapons and other plans, this time armed by Saddam," Bush said. It was frightening, but the fear was of something we were imagining ourselves.

Without really saying why, Bush compares Hussein to Hitler. He uses the words *terror* and *terrorism* interchangeably. He speaks of a "war on terror," so it won't seem so far from there to a war on Iraq.

He uses the words *free* and *freedom* a lot, to make the cause sound noble. But what does freedom have to do with it really? Terrorists hate us, not, as Bush once said, because we are free. They hate us because they see us as arrogant and selfish bullies.

There's no real proof, but even if the Iraqi leader is as dangerous as Bush says, that nevertheless does not explain why war is the only answer. Won't that lead to more hate, more fear, more weapons and more terrorism?

The "state of the onion," someone quipped, and like most jokes, this one has a serious side. When you peel off one by one the layers of Bush's argument, there's nothing left in your hand. There's no center, no core, just a strong smell. Next thing you know, you're crying.

2/4/03

On the Sick List

I*'ve not been writing* my column lately. I've
been sick. Not from sinusitis, SARS or spring fever.
Sick at heart. Sick at my stomach.

I'm sick of television pictures of bombs falling and
buildings burning. You can argue about it till you're
blue in the face, but all you have to do is look at the
pictures to know that war is hell.

I'm sick of what I see, and sicker of what I don't
see but know is there – the suffering of Iraqis, ordinary
people like you and me, killed, maimed, burned, terri-
fied, driven from their homes. Half a world away, I can
still hear babies crying. I can see the fear in the old
people's faces. The screams of children wake me up at
night.

I'm sick of hearing, "It's war. Of course there'll
be civilian casualties. Of course there'll be collateral
damage." As if naming it lessens the suffering – or the
blame.

I'm sick of the idea that we should be proud of all
this, proud of the fact that we, the biggest, richest and
most powerful nation on earth can march in and take
over a small weak country the size of California.

I'm sick of the idea that anybody who questions
the necessity, the morality or the legality of this war is
unpatriotic. I love my country, and I support the troops.
I want them to come home, play with their children,
grow old and die in their beds.

I'm sick when I think that, despite repeated pleas from American scholars to secure it, we set the stage for the trashing of Iraq's National Museum. Much of the looting, we now know, was carried out by professional art thieves, who apparently put a lot more thought than we did into what was going to happen after the tanks rolled into Baghdad. The priceless irreplaceable art objects and antiquities that were lost, many of them forever, represented not just the history and culture of Iraq, but of all of civilization. If there was a Garden of Eden, they say, it was there.

I'm sick of yellow ribbons, which flutter cheerfully from every mail box on my road. It's not just that they bring back a very bad Tony Orlando and Dawn song from the 1970s. It's that they tell a lie. They're misery and destruction, set to a catchy tune. They make us think that war is about love and loyalty and home-comings. War is about death. A bloody rag would be a better symbol.

I'm sick of hearing that this is all foretold in the Bible, that it's God's will, that it marks the beginning of the end of time. People have been saying that same thing for at least two thousand years. I wouldn't hold my breath.

4/21/03

my pinion bout the lection

Well the lection is over with and i am glad of it got to were you could not turn on the television without them yammer yammer yammer i did not vote for neither one of them i did not vote for ole Muley Face and i did not vote for ole Beady Eyes neither my daddy he wood not cast a vote unless he was to get payed for it and he stuck by that all his life and never wavered from that principle now he is gone and i left here by myself to carry on in the old timey ways they said on the television they was millions upon millions spent on the lection said bush spent more to get elected than ever been spent before but they was not much money changed hands round here this time i guess we will haf to wait for the local lections to see the money begin to circulate and the economy pick up around here i saw bush on the tv he said where he won so big he was going to do just what he pleased from now on well fifty-one percent i don't call that so big but he says it is and seem like if he says the same thing right over and over enough times the people will believe it now he says he will turn loose and do just like he wants to Lord if he has been holding back before now i hate to think. he will haf to start two or three big wars and run up a blue million dollars dett just to outdo hisself he said he had a man date but i thout he was against that he is a married man and that is what they jumped all over Bill Clinton at least he was with a womern but on the man

date now i don't hold it against them if that is what they
wont to do and not hurt nobody and i leave it up to the
lord if it is a sinn or not and not get mixed up were not
my business all i can do to keep my own self in line
much less everbody else the ones I know that is turned
like that they just want to be aloud to live in peace like
everbody else but now the preachers has got into it and
got the people all stirred up and i say it was all a trick
and a made up business to get the people all excited
afraid a big gang of lesbians about to come over the hill
and so they be shore to get out and vote and while they
was in there pull the lever and vote the bunn and the
bush back in office what did they ever do for anybody
hit is against the law for a preacher to tell the church
how to vote but now some of them does it or they will
hint around about it which amounts to the same thing a
preacher ort to abide by the law preach the word and let
the people decide how they will vote the politicians and
the preachers gets the people scared enough they will do
everwhat they tell them to and not stop and think about
it for theirselves why do they think the Lord give them a
brain in their head? they will vote how they are told to
vote not me tho i am sticking to my beliefs i will haf to
git payed

12/7/04

Simple Things:
The Mind of George Bush

I like the President, George W. Bush. A lot of people I know don't like him, can't even stand the sight of him. But I like him. He thinks the way I do – simple, not too complicated. That's how I like things to be – simple – and that's the way George likes them, too. With George, it's all this way or it's all that way, good or bad, right or wrong, now or never, us or them.

A lot of people that have been to college and read a lot of big heavy books about the history and the politics and the religion and the human behavior and so on, they don't see it like that. They're always complaining the world is not that simple. Well, the world might not be that simple but I am. I am a simple minded person and George W. Bush is the president for me.

Now I know he went to a big fancy school up north, Yale or somewhere, but they said he never studied much while he was up there, just laid around drunk, so he never did absorb any complicated information or knowledge that might have proved burdensome later.

Another thing I like about George W. Bush: once he makes up his mind, that's it. He sticks to his guns, buddy. Even when proved dead wrong again and again and again and again, he never gives it a second thought.

There was a third point I was aiming to make

about why I like George W Bush, but I forget what it was. Oh yes, I remember now. W stands for winner and George W Bush is a winner. I said before the election that there was no way on God's green earth that W was going to lose the election, and sure enough he didn't. He was willing to go the distance, give 110% and do whatever it took to win.

I ran into a buddy of mine at town the other day. He was all worried and upset, afraid somebody was about to come and take his Bible away from him right out of his pickup truck. I said I didn't think that was going to happen, that maybe he was worried about the wrong things. He said it surely was the truth because his brother-in-law from West Virginia had told him, plus they were talking about it up at the church house.

I suggested he might want to investigate some other sources of information, and that in fact I had heard that the Bush campaign had circulated false rumors before the election in West Virginia and Arkansas, claiming that the Democrats were about to take everybody's Bibles away. Which was ridiculous, of course, but they said it so people would get all nervous and afraid and run in there and vote the straight Republican ticket.

But they didn't circulate those rumors in Kentucky. I guess they figured we were too smart here in Kentucky to fall for a trick like that. Either that or they knew they'd win Kentucky anyway and didn't have to bother. So they put out this false rumor in Arkansas and West Virginia, and it just now making it to Kentucky. We always get everything after everybody else does.

Of course my friend didn't believe me. People believe what they want to, I guess. But some things are true whether you want to believe them or not.

That's another thing I like about George W. Bush. He's smart but not too smart. He's just smart enough to get in office.

1/20/05

Social Insecurity

Well, that is a relief anyhow. The president says if you are already on Social Security or will be before long, that you don't have to worry about this new business he's wanting to put in.

And I am glad of that. For as far as I can make out, what he wants to do is have people, instead of just getting a check every month like they have been doing, he wants them to take and put part of it in the stock market and see if it won't make more.

I can see it now – a lot of elderly and disabled around here that otherwise would have been on Social Security will be cruising up and down the road in fine automobiles, wearing designer clothes and smoking fat cigars where they have made a killing on Wall Street. We all know if there's anything you can depend on in this life it's the stock market.

The president likes to let on like he is just a regular fellow, but now I believe he may be overestimating the interest that the average Social Security recipient has in investing on Wall Street. The only thing most of us ever heard about investing is something like, "Honey, you need to invest in you a good pair of shoes." We don't know too much about a stock market, unless it's that place over behind the old Dairy Dart at London where you can go on Tuesday and sell a calf.

The president seems to think that people would enjoy getting to "shop" for their retirement plan and "shop" for their health insurance plan and "shop" for their investment portfolio. Shoot, I don't even like to go to town.

My opinion, most people would a heap rather just get their check out of the mailbox and go to the store and pick up the items that they need and come on back to the house and not have to fool with the stock market.

Just thinking about that type of thing can bore you silly or give you the swim-head inside of two minutes. I don't know about you, but if I am going to go to the trouble of thinking about something, I want to think about something interesting and important, like God, a good dog, or what are we going to fix for supper?

The president claims he has to change Social Security or it will go broke in abut forty years. Well, I appreciate his concern, since he is the one that has run the country in the hole, but others that have studied the matter and know a lot more about it than I do, they say that the Social Security system is not about to blow up any more than those weapons of mass destruction he had us all so worked up about a while back.

I have read that all this talk about changing Social Security is part of a plan some Republicans have to get rid of Social Security altogether. They don't like it. They're afraid people on Social Security are laying around living the life of Riley while they are doing all the work. They like to say, "Everybody has to stand on their own two feet."

But some people don't have two good feet. Plus, the older you get, the harder it gets to stand up for long periods of time without leaning on something. And around here, we've not got that many places to stand.

I guess President Bush and his rich friends don't have to worry about that. They won't ever need Social Security. But unless you're as rich as the Bush family, you never know when you or your family might be the ones that do.

4/7/05

In Search of the Liberal Agenda

I *have been hearing* a big lot of talk here lately about this liberal agenda. It's liberal agenda this and liberal agenda that every time you turn around. If a person did not know better they would think that the liberals were in power in this country and actually HAD an agenda. HA! HA! That was a good one.

Now I did not know what to think about all this talk about the liberal agenda, because I have been a liberal a long time now and proud of it and I know a big lot of good Christian people who are liberals also and no contradiction in that. I have been to a big lot of liberal-type meetings and gatherings and get-togethers, chanted liberal slogans, sung liberal songs, put on liberal T-shirts, eat liberal snacks, got my name on the mailing list and subscribed to the newsletter. But I must have been in the bathroom or outside smoking a cigarette when they passed out the agenda, because I never did get a copy and to tell the truth I never did see nor hear tell of any liberal agenda till right here lately.

So I decided to investigate around and see what I could find out about it. Naturally I went to that fount of all knowledge and information, the Internet. I surfed around on the World Wide Web for two days and three nights, till I was hump-backed, bleary-eyed, smelt bad, and begin to feel like I had been repeatedly knocked off my surfboard and drug around the ocean floor. But I am back now and all right and here are my findings and conclusions.

There are more than two thousand Web sites about the "liberal agenda." More than a thousand of these, or nearly one-half, are made up of conservatives' ideas about the liberal agenda.

The second biggest category – approximately one-fourth – is comprised of liberals making fun of conservatives' ideas about the liberal agenda.

Almost as many, about twenty per cent, are devoted to actual, serious liberal agendas. But they are all in other countries. Australia, India, Brazil, England, Canada, Ireland, New Zealand and the Philippines apparently have liberal agendas, but I couldn't find one for the United States, except for one county in California, and some guy in Milwaukee.

Many of the conservative sites claimed to have spotted "the liberal agenda" in Hollywood, in the media, and in churches, schools, and libraries. A surprisingly large number thought they detected a liberal agenda in the Bush administration.

The remaining sites tended to defy categorization. I am not sure what they were trying to say, and I don't think they were, either. But whatever it was, they seemed to have strong feelings about it.

The conservative sites had some mean and nasty things to say about their fellow Americans, but their views can be summarized as follows: some conservatives think that liberals are in league with the Devil, and that when liberals say they love God, love America, or care about children, the elderly, the poor, and the Bill of Rights, these are actually liberal code words meaning they hate God, hate America, despise children, the poor and the elderly, and are sick and tired of the Bill of Rights.

I found all of this surprising, to say the least, but I guess I shouldn't have. Asking conservatives about "the liberal agenda" is like asking an atheist about religion, or a confirmed bachelor about marriage. For one thing, they do not have a clue on the subject, and to make matters worse, they are trying to win you over to their point of view.

Many conservative sites sound sort of hysterical about "the liberal agenda" and it's hard to understand why. Conservatives have now captured the Presidency, both Houses of Congress, and an increasing number of judgeships in the country, including those on the Supreme Court. Conservatives control more state governorships and state legislatures than in decades, and fundamentalist and evangelical churches are growing so fast, some of them are called "mega-churches." Conservative commentators dominate radio and television talk shows, and are well represented in the print media. So it's hard to see why they insist on feeling paranoid and persecuted.

The only thing I can figure is, they must enjoy it. Maybe they can get more worked up if they feel like they've got some big booger enemy out there, instead of just a bunch of people who happen not to agree with them on everything. Or maybe they think they can get more converts that way. Now who is it again, that has the agenda?

Another thing I conclude is that while the Internet is indeed a great fount of knowledge and information, it is also a great fount of misinformation and, if you will excuse the expression, b#!!x^*+. Sadly, some people can't seem to tell the difference.

8/4/05

❦

Lighten Up, People

O*kay.* **Let's all try to relax.** Everybody take
a deep breath. In with the good air, out with the bad.
In with the good energy, out with the bad. There, that's
better.

Okay, I'm calling it. Right here, right now, right
by myself out behind the smokehouse on Teges Creek,
just me, God Almighty, fifteen dogs and maybe a copper-
head or two, I am calling for an end to the craziness.

By the last sentence of the first paragraph, the
reader should have a clear idea as to your topic. But
here we are, you and me, already well into the third
paragraph, and still I have not made plain what kind of
craziness I am wanting to put an end to, there being so
many different types and categories to pick from – from
the good old-fashioned kinds of craziness we had when
we were kids, to the scary new types that young persons
are always coming up with.

Friends, the kind of craziness I am concerned
about today is the kind that is making people act so
mad and hateful whenever they come up on something
they disagree with.

Seem like it has got to where you cannot even ex-
press your opinion on anything of a vaguely religious or
political nature, without having your intelligence, your
morals, and the final destination of your immortal soul
called into serious question.

Disagreeing with somebody is not necessarily a

bad thing. If the Lord had wanted us to agree on everything, he would have made us all just alike, and I reckon He could have done it like that if He'd a wanted to.
He must like to shake it up. I guess He's easy bored.
Because He made such an astonishing variety of plants
and animals and people and so on. It's hard to remember, but we need to bear in mind that the Creator of
the Universe is not necessarily a white male Protestant
Republican from Southeastern Kentucky.

The trouble doesn't come from people disagreeing. Good people, sincere people, smart people can
see things different ways. It depends on our personal-
ity, how we were brought up, the people we've met, the
books we've read, the experiences we've had.

Disagreement can be a good thing. But there are
ways to disagree, and ways not to. You can disagree
with somebody without getting mad, giving them down
the road and calling them everything but a milk cow.

And if you are going to write in to the newspaper
about something, for the love of Mike, stick to the subject. Don't go around Robin Hood's barn talking about
abortion and the Holocaust and first one thing and then
another and everything from soup to hay. Just state
your opinion and give your reasons. You don't have to
act ugly about it.

I blame a lot of this on TV. Maybe we should all
turn off the television and go set on the porch or read
a book. FOX, CNN, NBC, CBS, ABC, XYZ – I wouldn't
give you a nickel for any of them. They all get people
on there to holler and shout and interrupt one another.
They don't go into depth on anything and they don't
tell us what is really going on. They just want to make
money, so they show us a fight, we pick a side, and then
we start acting the same way – loud, rude, intolerant,
and mad as a wet hen.

The news stations seem to think we are all dumb
as a tick and have the attention span of a flea. (Forgive
the canine metaphors. We write what we know.) And so
rudeness is spreading across our nation like the mange.

We must stop this before it turns to violence, before our democracy is threatened, and before all the hair falls out. We must administer the mange medicine of mutual respect. We must dip the dog in tolerance.

Well, you get my point.

6/02/05

Religion

THE APOSTLE PAUL
NEVER SAID ANYTHING ABOUT
WOMEN KEEPING SILENT
IN THE NEWSPAPER

Visit to a Little Country Church

The other Sunday I went with a friend of mine to her church.

It was a beautiful Lord's Day morning, the sun warm on the hills and fields, the air alive with birdsong, heavy with honeysuckle.

We got to the church house and there was a good crowd there. Some of them turned and smiled at us when we came in. Babies fussed; little girls roamed the aisles in organza dresses; little boys crawled under the pews to play with toy trucks.

We sang some good old hymns, bowed our heads in prayer, passed the offering plate, and settled in to hear a good sermon.

And then I swear if that preacher didn't get up in the pulpit and preached for a solid forty-five minutes and never talked about a thing in the world but sodomy.

Now I don't know about you, but I don't find the thoughts of two men going at it all that spiritually in-spiring. So having nothing better to do, I passed the time by trying to figure out why a preacher would find this topic so intriguing.

I looked around at the congregation – young mar-ried couples, widows, people who had been married forty or fifty years. People who were going to go home, eat dumplings and banana pudding, visit with their fami-lies, maybe work in the garden a while in the evening. They did not appear to be a crowd that was teetering on the brink of some dangerous homosexual activity.

That preacher quoted the Bible, but surely he knew that the Bible talks a lot more about fornication and adultery and a lot of other sins than it does about homosexuality, which is not included in the Ten Commandments, and which Jesus never mentioned once, him being not nearly so judgmental as a lot of Christians are.

The sermon drew a few hearty *Amen's*, more than you'd get, probably, from preaching love, forgiveness, justice, mercy, giving to him that asketh of thee, and turning the other cheek.

Like a lot of churches around here, this one set in the middle of a pot patch. In the shadow of its steeple were some of the poorest people and some of the heaviest drug traffic in the nation. But the church, equipped with an elaborate security system, seemed designed, both physically and theologically, to keep these people out. Maybe there were other Bible messages we needed to hear.

My friends who are gay tell me God made them that way, and I believe them.

But even if you insist on seeing gays and lesbians as sinners, they are going to have to get in line with all the rest of us sinners – fornicators, adulterers, judgers, gossips and hypocrites. It's going to be a long line. And nobody better pick up a rock.

6/2/03

Women in the Bible

I'm glad I don't have to depend on some of these men preachers for all of my information about the Bible. For if I did, the only women in the Bible I'd be likely to ever hear about would be Eve, Ruth, Jezebel, and the Virgin Mary.

Eve and Jezebel were not too good a role models, and of course it would take a miracle to be as good as the Virgin Mary. So that leaves just Ruth, the good daughter-in-law, to study and try to emulate.

Fortunately there are a lot more women in the Bible, women who were strong, brave, wise, and filled with the spirit. It's just that you don't hear much about them for some reason.

You don't hear about Shiphrah and Puah, for example, the midwives who defied the Pharaoh's order to destroy Hebrew babies at birth (Exodus 1:15-24).

You don't hear about Deborah, a prophet and one of the twelve judges of Israel, who planned a military campaign and led her people into battle (Judges 4).

You don't hear about the prophet Huldah, whom the King of Israel consulted to learn the will of God (2 Kings 22:14-20).

The Bible says Moses' sister Miriam was also a prophet. After the crossing of the Red Sea, she played the tambourine and danced in thanksgiving to God (Exodus 15:20-21).

You don't hear much about Esther, either, though

there's a whole Old Testament book about her. It tells the story of a Jewish woman who became Queen and saved her people from oppression and death.

In the New Testament, the prophet Anna recognized the Christ in the infant Jesus (Luke 2:36-38).

You hear a lot about what the Apostle Paul said about women. But mostly what you hear is just how they should keep their hair long, be subservient to their husbands and keep quiet in the church.

You don't hear so much about Phoebe, whom Paul identifies as a deacon in the early church (Romans 16:1). Some translations say *servant*, *deaconess*, or *minister*, but the Greek word means *deacon*.

We've all heard of Peter, Barnabas and Stephen. But what about Tabitha (Acts 9:36), Lydia (Acts 16:40), Priscilla (Romans 16:3), Lois and Eunice (2 Timothy 1:5)?

Mary Magdalene, Joanna, Susanna, and many other women traveled with Jesus from place to place and, we are told, supported Jesus' work out of their own means (Luke 8:1-3).

Jesus' women followers stood at the foot of his cross, were the first to witness his Resurrection, and, along with the twelve apostles and the brothers of Jesus, were present in the Upper Room at Pentecost (Acts 1:12-14, Acts 2:4).

"And ALL of them were filled with the Holy Spirit."

2/24/03

A Woman's Place

*T**he other day*** I was visiting a church in another county, and had the bad luck to be there when they were having their annual business meeting. A few men seemed to be running the show, trying to fill various committees for the coming year. The trouble was, there weren't many people there, and nobody that seemed much interested in being on a committee.

So to solve that problem, one of the men got the bright idea they would just "appoint" some of the women to a committee, since the women, presumably, would do it whether they wanted to or not.

Well, most of the women were down in the fellowship hall trying to warm up about eighty-five casseroles for the dinner. The ones that had the misfortune to be trapped in the business meeting started trying to hide behind the people in the pews in front of them so they wouldn't have to be on a committee.

Nevertheless, the very idea of women on committees seemed to make one of the men nervous, and he got up and made a big long speech, totally without provocation or encouragement of any kind, about how women shouldn't be on committees at all. Not that they wouldn't actually do a better job than the men, he added, and nobody argued with him there.

But it was against the Bible, he said, and it was untelling what Old Testament-type plagues might be unleashed if a woman was to serve on a committee.

71

First of all, he said, though nobody was asking him, it was against the Book of Genesis, which clearly states that when God created man and woman, He created the woman out of the man's body as a helpmeet. What that means, he went on to explain, though nobody asked him, was that man was supposed to be dominant over woman, just like he was over the animals.

Then, as further evidence that it is wrong and bad and sinful for women to be on committees, he skips from the creation story in Genesis all the way over to I Timothy – bypassing the rest of the Pentateuch, the Prophets, the Psalms and the gospels – and lands heavily on the verse where the Apostle Paul states that the women should "be in silence."

I wished I'd had my Bible with me, the big annotated one, with notes, concordance, maps, helps and aids. I believe I'd have throwed it right at his pointy head. So I guess it's just as well I didn't have it with me.

What I really wished is that I could stand up and make a speech in answer to his. But since women aren't allowed to speak up in that church, I didn't get to. So I just went meekly down to the fellowship hall and got in line for the casseroles. But if I could have made a speech, here's what I'd have said. (I don't believe the Apostle Paul said anything about women keeping silent in the newspaper.)

First of all, I'd tell him, people who actually study the Bible, and don't just go through it looking for reasons to keep women off committees, know that there are two different accounts of creation in Genesis, and that they are quite different from one another.

In Genesis 1, God works for six days and creates, in this order, water, light, sky, land, plants, sun, moon, stars, birds, fish, and animals. Then "God created man in his own image, in the image of God he created him; male and female he created them" (Genesis 1:27). In this version, God creates man and woman at the same time. Then, His work finished, he rests on the seventh day.

The other account, which begins with Genesis 2:4, is not a summary, but a different version. And since it differs from the previous version in both style and content, it was probably written by a different author.

In this version of the creation, God creates the earth first, then water, then man, then plants and animals, and then woman, from the body of Adam.

So we have two quite different accounts, both of the order of creation and of the creation of woman. The contradiction doesn't bother me, but it ought to bother you, I'd tell him, since you're the one who claims to take the Bible literally. Both versions can't be right. Which one are you going to pick?

Wait. Don't tell me. You're going to pick the one you like better, the one where God makes woman out of Adam's rib, just to help Adam out, and sort of as an afterthought.

Well, if you can pick one and let the other one go, so can I. I like the first one, the one where God creates them male and female, at the same time, and equal.

As for I Timothy 2:12, where the women are told "not to usurp authority over the man, but to be in silence," we have all heard this verse all our lives. It is surely one of the most popular verses in the Bible, particularly among men, who are encouraged to memorize it, along with football plays, from an early age.

Most of them probably couldn't quote you more than three or four of the Beatitudes, the Ten Commandments or the Seven Sayings of Christ on the Cross, but they can quote Timothy 2:12 till the cows come home.

It's no surprise Paul saw women the way he did. Paul's Epistles may have been inspired by God, but that doesn't mean they were dictated word for word, like a boss dictating to a secretary.

Paul was bound to reflect some of his own ideas and the ideas of his time. And in Paul's time, not only could women not own property; women WERE property.

But Paul does contradict himself on the subject. 1 Corinthians 11:5 assumes that women will be pray-

ing and prophesying in the church. You can pray silent-
ly, but to prophesy you just about have to open your
mouth.

Another verse you don't hear near as much as you
do the one about keeping silent is Galatians 3:28:
"... there is neither male nor female: for ye are all one in
Christ Jesus."

10/25/01

~~

Fussin' about the Bible

I was trying to find some good music on the radio the other day and was not having too much luck, seem like, when I came across a station where some people were talking about something or another, and whatever it was, you could tell they were against it. I decided to listen a while and see what it was that had them people so worked up.

Come to find out it was the Bible. Somebody was about to come out with a new translation, and these people did not like it one bit. They hadn't actually read it yet, but they could already tell they didn't like it.

What they were talking about is a new translation of the New Testament called *Today's New International Version,* or TNIV for short. The new version is a revision of the respected and popular *New International Version,* or NIV.

Only about seven percent of the new TNIV is different from the NIV, and less than a third of those changes have to do with gender. But since those are the ones that seem to upset people the most for some reason, let's take a look at three typical examples.

First, Luke 17:3. In the NIV this verse was translated from the Greek like this: "If your brother sins, rebuke him, and if he repents, forgive him." The NIV translated the Greek word *adelphos* as *brother.* But in Greek that word has no gender. It can mean males, females or both. Since both men and women sin and need rebuking and forgiving, and since the Greek word can be translated either way, the TNIV translates it here as *brother* or *sister* instead of just *brother*. "If any brother or sister sins against you, rebuke the offender; and if they repent, forgive them." This is more accurate than the previous translation, since it more clearly reflects the original meaning of the verse.

The NIV translated John 6:35 this way: "Then Jesus declared, 'I am the bread of life. He who comes to me will never go hungry, and he who believes in me will never be thirsty.'" Where the NIV translated the Greek pronoun as *he*, the TNIV translates it as *whoever*. Either translation is equally correct, but since Jesus invites everyone to come unto him, the new version reflects the meaning of the passage more clearly: "Then Jesus declared, 'I am the bread of life. Whoever comes to me will never go hungry, and whoever believes in me will never be thirsty.'"

Romans 3:28 in the NIV read: "For we maintain that a man is justified by faith apart from observing the law." The NIV translated the Greek word *anthropos* as *man*, which is correct. But it is just as correct and actually more common to translate it as *person*. In this case *person* is a better translation because this verse applies to everybody. So the TNIV reads: "For we maintain that a person is justified by faith, apart from observing the law."

Looking at these examples, it's hard to see what all the fuss is about. Changes like these do not change the meaning of the Biblical passages. They make that meaning more clear.

So why were those people on the radio so upset? I think they suffered from a lack of information.

They seemed not to understand that all Bibles in English are translations, and that translating is not as simple a process as trading out parts in a machine. Words, phrases and sentences can be translated a number of different ways. Teams of scholars spend years poring over various manuscripts, versions, translations and dictionaries. That's how we got the King James, and that's how we got the NIV.

The people on the radio seemed not to understand that the people who work on translating the Bible are not trying to be "politically correct" or to make a lot of money off the Scriptures. They are trying to come up with the best translation they can, to make it as clear and as close to the original meaning as possible.

The truths of the Bible do not change. But since language does change, we need a new translation every so often, so that we can read the Bible in the language we speak now.

We don't say *men* or *mankind* anymore when we mean *all of humanity*, and that's a good thing. Most men probably wouldn't have put up with it near this long if they'd been told that whenever we meant everybody we were just going to say *woman*.

When we're talking about men, let's say so. When we're talking about women, let's say that. When we're talking about everybody, let's make that plain.

That's what the TNIV does and we ought to welcome it. It will be good for girls growing up in the church to know for sure that the message of the Bible applies just as much to them.

2/28/02

A Wet Week at Bible Camp

Didn't it rain, children, didn't it rain. It rained early. It rained late. It rained buckets, cats and dogs. It rained forty days and forty nights. It rained on the hills and the valleys, on the roads and the fields, on the just and the unjust and those holding wet newspapers over their heads.

The rain in Spain may stay mainly in the plain, but here it washed gravel out of driveways, covered low-water bridges, and formed shallow lakes at the lower ends of vegetable gardens and tobacco patches. The rains came down and the floods came up.

In fact it rained so much last week at Faith Christian Assembly Youth Camp, we had to remind ourselves of God's promise to Noah in Genesis 9:15. The rain descended and the floods came and the winds blew and beat upon our cabins, but they fell not. The rain it raineth every day, but it raineth not on our parade.

In the mornings, the kids studied the Bible. In the midst of a green forest dripping rain from a million leaves, we huddled under shelters and talked about God's gifts. We talked about how we all have different gifts, and about how God wants us to use our gifts to help others. We talked about Christian love and tolerance and compassion. We joined hands and thanked God for all His gifts to us, including rain.

In the mornings they studied the Bible; in the afternoons, they played. They threw Frisbees in the rain. They went down the waterslide in the rain. They slid down mud banks on their rear ends in the rain. They got into water fights with water guns, water balloons and anything else that would hold water. Several showed promise of a bright future in mud wrestling.

When the bell rang to signal the end of "recreation time," they slogged back to their cabins, showered, blow-dried their hair and changed clothes, pinning their wet shorts and T-shirts to a clothesline behind the cabins, where they hung for days and never did get dry.

In the evenings, we had a campfire. If it was still raining or there wasn't enough dry wood, somebody put liquid fuel and a roll of toilet paper in a big tin can and we sat around that, singing, praying and listening to preaching. Several campers, dry for the first time that day, came forward to be baptized and were promptly immersed in the camp baptistery.

Last week the Lord sent an abundance of rain upon the earth, rain from heaven and fruitful seasons, filling our hearts with gladness. God gave us showers of blessing, enough to fill streams, grow crops and float boats, enough to play in, enough to drink of the water of life, enough to wash our sins away.

6/23/03

A Different Bible?

Well, **I am glad** to have that cleared up. It's good to get the paper every week so you can find out important stuff.

For example, in my ignorance I had always thought that if I ever got in a real bad way, if I was bad off sick, or got hurt and couldn't do for myself, or if I ever got to where I didn't have enough to feed my family, I could go to where the Christians were at and ask them for help. Because they are supposed to show Christian compassion and the love of Jesus and help the people that needs it.

And it made me feel better just to know that there are so many good Christians and so many churches around that would open up their hearts and maybe even their pocketbooks if I got to where I needed help. Now that is just what I always thought.

But after reading a column a preacher wrote in *The Manchester Enterprise* here a while back I see that I was badly fooled in my thinking about the church. Come to find out the church, at least to hear this one preacher tell it, is not a bit interested in my doctor bills or my employment situation or the nutritional needs of my children, but just in the state of my immortal soul. Well, I appreciate that, I do. I just always thought there was more to being a Christian than that. I guess I was misinformed.

I'd been under the impression that the church

from the very beginning and in all times and places has looked upon helping the poor as a big part of doing the Lord's work. But this preacher seemed to think it was just something a few churches started doing here lately to try to act modern and draw a big crowd. I always thought they were doing it to follow Christ's teachings, to relieve suffering, and to act out the love of God.

He said there are government programs to help people in need, and that's right, there are. But there's not near as many as there used to be, and they don't help near as much as people think they do. People that don't know think that people on welfare and food stamps have got it made. They frown in the checkout line if they see somebody buying a big lot or getting something they think they ought not to have, and them on food stamps.

But they don't know that person's heart and they don't know their life. They don't know but what that person might not have been to the store for a solid month, and that what they got the last time just lasted about two weeks. They don't know how many people they've got to feed nor who's sick at that house nor anything about it, they just think they do.

That preacher said that the Bible doesn't authorize the church to spend the Lord's money on helping the poor and needy. Well, I've read that book kiver to kiver myself and I can't find out where it authorizes the church to spend money on air conditioning, carpet and padded pews either but they do. The Bible as a whole seems a lot more concerned with brotherly love than it does with church budgetary matters.

And this preacher seemed to think that what the Bible tells individual Christians to do and what it tells the church to do are two different things. But I can't find that in there, either. I must have a different Bible or something. Here's what the one I've got says:

"Thou shalt open thine hand wide unto thy brother, to thy poor and to thy needy in thy land."
– Deuteronomy 15:11

"Blessed is he that considereth the poor: the LORD will deliver him in time of trouble." – Psalms 41:1

"Whoso stoppeth his ears at the cry of the poor, he also shall cry himself, but shall not be heard." – Proverbs 21:13

"Give to him that asketh thee, and from him that would borrow of thee turn not thou away." – Matthew 5:42

"But whoso hath this world's goods, and seeth his brother have need, and shutteth up his bowels of compassion from him, how dwelleth the love of God in him?" – I John 3:17

"What doth it profit, my brethren, though a man say he hath faith, and have not works? Can faith save him? If a brother or sister be naked, and destitute of daily food, And one of you say unto them, Depart in peace, be ye warmed and filled; notwithstanding ye give them not those things which are needful to the body; what doth it profit? Even so faith, if it hath not works, is dead, being alone." – James 2:14-17

"Then shall the King say unto them on his right hand, Come, ye blessed of my Father, inherit the kingdom prepared for you from the foundation of the world: For I was an hungred, and ye gave me meat: I was thirsty, and ye gave me drink: I was a stranger, and ye took me in: Naked, and ye clothed me: I was sick, and ye visited me: I was in prison, and ye came unto me.

"Then shall the righteous answer him, saying, Lord, when saw we thee an hungred, and fed thee? or thirsty, and gave thee drink? When saw we thee a stranger, and took thee in? or naked, and clothed thee? Or when saw we thee sick, or in prison, and came unto thee? And the King shall answer and say unto them, Verily I say unto you, Inasmuch as ye have done it unto one of the least of these my brethren, ye have done it unto me." – Matthew 25:34-40

8/15/02

Plowing the Middle Ground

Somebody made the statement the other day that you either accept the Bible as the word of God or you reject it, that there's no middle ground.

This is the type of statement that sounds right when you first hear it, but that really doesn't make a lick of sense.

Because if you think about it, there are miles and miles of middle ground between the two extremes of totally rejecting the Bible on the one hand, and on the other hand, accepting its every word as literal and inerrant truth, straight from the mouth of God.

And somewhere in that vast middle ground is where we all stand. We might not all stand in the same place. Some of us might be a little bit closer to one end or the other. But we all stand somewhere between those two extremes.

It's hard to find anybody who takes every word in the Bible as "the gospel truth," even if they say they do.

Some Christians think the Bible means exactly what it says when it says that believers "shall take up serpents; and if they drink any deadly thing, it shall not hurt them; they shall lay hands on the sick, and they shall recover" (Mark 16:18). But other Christians say this verse does not apply to believers today, that we are not supposed to take it literally.

Some Christians retain the New Testament practice of glossolalia, speaking in tongues (Acts 2:4). But others do not. They say this doesn't apply to us today, that we're not supposed to take that literally.

In the Sermon on the Mount, Jesus assumes that his followers will fast (Matthew 6:17). But few Christians today think this applies to them.

Jesus also preached against divorce (Matthew 5:32). A lot of us have had trouble taking that one literally.

Not many people take Jesus literally when he commanded us not to judge others (Matthew 7:1), but to forgive them (Matthew 6:14-15), to love our enemies (Matthew 5:44), and to turn the other cheek (Matthew 5:39).

Some preachers tend to steer away from Jesus' teachings in the Sermon on the Mount and in the story of the Good Samaritan. By neglecting these passages, they imply that you can't really take Jesus literally.

Some preachers will go to great lengths to try to explain why the Bible doesn't mean what it says in Matthew 19:23, that "a rich man shall hardly enter into the kingdom of heaven."

You've got to analyze the context, they'll say. You have to understand the time and the place. You've got to consider who's being told this and why. You have to know something that's not in the Bible. You can't take it literally.

But when it comes to something else, like a passage that seems to restrict the role of women in the church, they become quite literal. In passages that seem to confirm their own view of how things ought to be, they make no allowance for history, for culture, for audience, or for varying translations and interpretations.

Different people and different churches may choose different parts of the Bible to take literally. Nobody seems to take it all that way.

I don't believe you'll find many people at the other extreme either. It's hard to find anybody who rejects the Bible completely.

Many Christians have studied the history of the Bible and do not believe it was dictated word for word by God Himself. But that doesn't mean they're throwing out the Bible. They're just looking at it differently.

Many Christians have studied the Bible and do not believe that a letter Paul wrote to a certain church in the first century was meant to apply to every church all over the world from then till the end of time.

But that doesn't mean they're rejecting the Bible. They're just looking at it differently.

They may place more authority on the teachings of Jesus, who put mercy before doctrine, and love of neighbor before the letter of the law.

Different people and different denominations look at the Bible and at particular passages in the Bible in different ways. And that's okay.

As long as we keep our hearts and our minds open. As long as we admit that we don't any of us know much. And as long as we respect the rights of others to believe and to worship in their own way.

11/22/01

That Old Time Religion

Gimme that old time religion, we sang in church last Sunday morning.

I looked around at the congregation and wondered what different things "the old time religion" meant to us. The religion we grew up with? The religion of our grandparents? Our great-grandparents? Gimme that old-time religion. It's good enough for me.

The religion of our grandparents and great-grandparents had some qualities that we should try very hard never to lose. We would be doing well to emulate the sincerity of their beliefs, the central role of religion in their lives, and the way they acted out the commandment to "love thy neighbor" by helping one another raise barns, crops and children.

But there are aspects of "the old time religion" that we have to question. God does not change and the Bible does not change, but this world does change, and it is in this world that we have to live and act out our faith. Some of the challenges we face as Christians today may be different from the challenges our grandparents faced, because, in some ways, we live in a different world.

The world our grandparents and great-grandparents knew was, for the most part, a small and familiar place. Most of their neighbors looked like them. They spoke the same way. They lived the same way. They ate the same things, and they believed the same things.

Most of our grandparents and great-grandparents, wise or good or intelligent as they may have been, had little understanding of – and little use for – people who were different from them.

Except for military duty and trips to the North to work, few had contact with people from other places, and even fewer had the opportunity to study and learn about other cultures. Their world was the community in which they lived and the similar communities that lay close by.

The world we inhabit now is wider and more varied. Transportation and technology put us in touch with people all over the planet. Global trade and global politics mean that what happens on the other side of the world affects us here, that what happens here affects folks everywhere.

More of us now travel to foreign countries, and more of us know people who have come from other countries to live here. They are our friends, our co-workers, our doctors, our students and teachers. They are our neighbors. And since God's word does not change, the commandment "love thy neighbor" still applies.

We talk about pluralism, multi-culturalism and tolerance. But I hope we are moving toward a time when we don't just "tolerate" people from different cultures and religions, but when we can appreciate and enjoy both the ways we are all different, and the ways we are all the same.

The two major world religions of Christianity and Islam, for example, though different, have a great deal in common. They worship the same God. Both sprang from the tradition of Abraham, within a few hundred years of each other, in the same region of the world. Both believe in heaven and hell, and both have holy texts, which they believe to have been given to them by God. In the family of world religions, they are first cousins.

Both Christianity and Islam have wide variations

within them. Just as Christianity embraces Roman Catholicism, Anglicanism, Eastern Orthodoxy, and hundreds of different Protestant denominations, Islam, too, takes various forms. In both religions the beliefs of followers may range from very conservative to very liberal, with many brands of moderates in between.

Both Christianity and Islam contain fundamentalist groups that represent the conservative extremes of both religions. Fundamentalists, in both Christianity and Islam, tend to take their holy texts very literally.

They believe that God has spoken to them and to them alone, that they and they alone know the will of God. They believe that they are totally right and that everyone else is totally wrong. They believe that God is always on their side.

Most Muslims and most Christians do not think this way. But tragically, this is the kind of thinking that, pushed to an extreme, led fundamentalist Islamic terrorists to attack the Pentagon and the World Trade Center, killing many innocent people. Sadly, it is also the kind of thinking that we sometimes hear in our own Christian churches and on supposedly Christian programs on television and radio.

But this kind of thinking represents neither the essence of Christianity nor what was best about "the old-time religion." God is surely bigger than any of us can begin to fathom. Rather than proclaiming our own omniscience, we should proclaim the omniscience of God and stand in awe before Him. Rather than condemning the beliefs of others, we should work and pray to be good Christians ourselves, and to love our neighbors – all of them.

10/11/01

Thou Shalt Not Display the Ten Commandments in the Courthouse

***T**he U.S. Supreme Court* recently ruled that displays of the Ten Commandments in the McCreary and Pulaski County (Kentucky) courthouses are unconstitutional.

I disagree with the Supreme Court sometimes, but I'm going to have to go along with them on this one. Here's why:

Reason #1 -- Separation of church and state

Some people think that if you're against putting the Ten Commandments in the courthouse or the public schools, you're against religion. But that's not true. I'm FOR religion, and that's why I don't want the government messing around with it.

The people who founded our country had experienced religious persecution in England, and they wanted to make sure it didn't happen here. They wanted Americans to be free to worship as they wanted, without interference from the government. They built into our Constitution what Thomas Jefferson called a "wall of separation between church and state." As long as this wall stands, the government cannot forbid religion, promote religion, or favor one religion over another. For more than two centuries, this wall has afforded us a degree of religious peace and freedom unheard of in much of the rest of the world and in all of history before us. We had better not start pulling stones out of it.

Let's let the church do its job, and the government try to do its, and not let them stick their noses in one another's business. Or, as James Madison put it, "Religion and government will both exist in greater purity, the less they are mixed together."

Reason #2 – Freedom of religion

A lot of these Ten Commandments monuments have been around a long time. Some were erected in the 1950s when the movie came out where Charlton Heston played Moses. Why are they controversial now?

It's not because there's some big conspiracy against religion. It's because the United States has become more religiously diverse.

Three out of four Americans identify themselves as Christians. That means that one out of four Americans is non-religious, or belongs to another religious tradition – Judaism, Islam, Buddhism or Hinduism, to name just the big four.

In elections and referendums, the majority rules. But our democracy guarantees certain rights, not only to the majority, but to the minority, too. "All men are created equal," and all American citizens, regardless of race, gender, color, creed, religion, or national origin, are equally entitled to the rights and freedoms our Constitution guarantees, including freedom of religion.

So I can understand why, as American citizens and taxpayers, non-Christians might resent finding a Christian text or Christian symbols in a public place. If the shoe were on the other foot, would we want our tax money spent on a statue of Buddha? Would we want to be greeted by a passage from the Koran every time we go to get our license tags renewed?

In a democracy, we have an understanding. I may not agree with you, but I respect your freedoms and you respect mine. That way, we can all stay free.

Reason #3. The arguments in favor of posting the Ten Commandments in public places aren't all that convincing.

Some people say the Ten Commandments should be displayed in courthouses because they form the foundation of the American legal system. But our legal system derives from many other sources as well, and half the commandments are clearly religious rather than ethical.

Other people think that having the Ten Commandments around where everybody could see them would make things better, but I'm not sure it would.

Maybe they want to take us back to a time when people knew the Ten Commandments and kept them, a time when things were better and nicer than they are now. I'm not sure that time ever really existed, and even if it did, tacking a list of ancient Jewish laws on the wall isn't going to bring it back. Things just aren't that simple.

The Ten Commandments themselves aren't all that simple, either. They come from a time and a culture very different from our own. They say nothing about abortion, homosexuality, or many of the other issues we struggle with today. They accept slavery. They refer to women as property. "Honor they father and mother" is good advice. I'm not sure how much it would mean to a boy whose mother abandoned him or a girl whose father abused her. And few Christians observe the commandments about graven images, meaning statues, or keeping Saturday, the Sabbath Day, holy.

The King James Bible has three different versions of the Ten Commandments (Exodus 20:2-17, Exodus 34:12-26, and Deuteronomy 5:6-21). The Hebrew, Christian and Islamic versions are all different, and the Roman Catholic version is different from the Protestant. To post one version rather than another in a government building implies that the government endorses one religion or denomination over another, and the government can't do that.

Nobody is trying to take the Ten Commandments away. If you want to read, memorize, discuss, and follow the Ten Commandments, teach them to your children, and display them on church or private property – go to it! Nobody's trying to stop you. If anybody did try, the American Civil Liberties Union would be the first ones there to fight for your right to keep them. This argument is not about "activist judges" or some imagined conspiracy to undermine religion. It's about the Constitution and the Bill of Rights.

Instead of raising a ruckus about posting the Ten Commandments in government buildings, maybe we should just work harder on observing them ourselves.

And we might flip over to the New Testament once in a while, too, and re-read what Jesus said in Matthew 7:12 and 22:36-40.

7/7/05

The Ten Commandments of Jesus

"If Jesus came back** and saw what was being done in his name, he'd never stop throwing up."

I didn't write that line. Somebody else did. But they've got a point.

It's interesting how little attention we pay to the things Jesus actually said when he walked the earth, even those of us who call ourselves Christians, who profess to believe that Jesus was the Son of God, and who attend churches that bear his name.

If you just went by what most Christians do and what they talk about, in the church and out, you'd get the idea that after Jesus was born of the Virgin Mary, he just sat around the house for thirty-two years, passing the time and waiting to get crucified.

Jesus actually had quite a bit to say about things, but we don't hear too much about it. We hear a lot more about what the Apostle Paul said than we do about what Jesus himself said. And we talk a lot more about other religious topics.

We talk about how often to take communion, which translation of the Bible to read, what kind of music to play in church, how much water it takes to get baptized. We argue about how long it took God to make the world, when the Judgment Day's a-coming, and who ought to be allowed to accept the call to preach. Why do we pay so much more attention to all these other things than we do to what Jesus actually said?

Maybe it's just easier. Maybe it's easier to criticize other denominations and other religions than to try to live by the Sermon on the Mount. Maybe it's easier to hair-split the Bible, like lawyers over a law book, than to follow the Golden Rule.

We like to condemn those who say that Jesus was a great teacher, because as Christians we believe he was much more than that. But does that mean we can turn around and ignore Christ's teachings?

We like to emphasize that we are saved by faith and by grace, and not by works. But does that mean we don't have to obey Christ's instructions to perform good works?

If we could ever summon the courage and the faith to really follow the teachings of Jesus, we could transform our lives and our communities. We could transform the world.

But so far most of us haven't shown that much faith or that much courage. Our failure to do so is what keeps people away from our churches. It opens us up to the charge of hypocrisy, and until we do better, I'm afraid the charge is true.

In the Sermon on the Mount in Matthew chapters 5 through 7, Jesus told us that we ought to obey the laws of Moses, but he also told us that we have to go beyond the law. Instead of arguing about whether to display the Ten Commandments in public buildings, maybe we ought to just quietly carry around in our pocket or purse a copy of some of the commandments of Jesus, and pull them out and read them every once in a while, to see how we're doing. Here are ten from the Sermon on the Mount.

Jesus' Ten Commandments

1. Let your light so shine before men, that they may see your good works, and glorify your Father which is in heaven.

2. Swear not at all, but let your communication be Yea, yea, Nay, nay.

3. Resist not evil: but whosoever shall smite thee on thy right cheek, turn to him the other also.

4. Whosoever shall compel thee to go a mile, go with him two.

5. Give to him that asketh of thee, and from him that would borrow of thee, turn thou not away.

6. Love your enemies, bless them that curse you, do good to them that hate you, and pray for them which despitefully use you and persecute you.

7. Forgive men their trespasses, for then your heavenly Father will also forgive you. But if you forgive men not their trespasses, neither will your Father forgive your trespasses.

8. Take no thought, saying, What shall we eat? or, What shall we drink? or, With what shall we be clothed? But seek ye first the kingdom of God, and his righteousness; and all these things shall be added unto you.

9. Judge not, that you be not judged.

10. In all things whatsoever you would that men should do to you, do you even so to them: for this is the law and the prophets.

1/24/02

᠊ᢍ

The Gays, the Bishops
and the Robinsons

*W*ell, *I imagine a lot of preachers* didn't
have to prepare a big lot for their sermons this past
Sunday. It was handed to them on a silver platter, sort
of like John the Baptist's head, only this time it was the
head of Gene Robinson, the gay Episcopal bishop.

I can just about hear them now. "First they took
prayer out of the schools. And everbody said, That's
all right-tuh. Then they took the Ten Commandments
down off the wall and threw them in the garbage can.
And everbody said, That's all right-tuh. And now we've
got women and homosexuals preaching from the pulpit.
And everbody says, That's all right-tuh. But church I
tell you today it's NOT all right-tuh! It's not all right-tuh
with the Bible! It's not all right-tuh with the Lord!! It's
not all right-tuh with the worda God-duh!!! How can
people that SAY THEY ARE A CHRISTIAN and READ
THE BIBLE and GO TO CHURCH ON SUNDAY, how can
they go along with having a HOMOSEXUAL be a LEAD-
ER in the CHURCH??? I don't understand it."

Well, I know you don't understand it, preacher,
but if you'll sit down and hush for a few minutes I'll try
to explain it to you.

They's a lot to it but it boils down to this. Are you
a Christ-centered Christian or a Bible-centered Christian?

A Bible-centered Christian says, Looky here it

says it in the Bible and that's hit, case closed.

But as anybody knows that's read it all the way through, the Bible's not that simple of a book. There's a whole lot in the Bible that applies to the times in which it was written, like about slavery and sacrificing animals and all types of things that reflect the culture and practices and prejudices of olden times. The Bible's got, not just God's word in there, it's got some of man's word in there, too.

The Bible wasn't dictated word for word by God Himself. People wrote it. And if God was working through them, He did it like He always does, through human beings, with all our faults and failings and prejudices. Some of those got in the Bible, just like they get in the church – through people.

A Christ-centered Christian can read the Bible and get a lot out of it. They can believe it was inspired by God. But they're going to look at the context, too. They're going to see those few verses about homosexuality as man's prejudice, not God's.

A Christ-centered Christian puts the most emphasis on the teachings of Christ. Jesus preached a message of love, inclusion and compassion. Of judge not that ye be not judged. Of get the log out of your own eye before you go after the speck of sawdust in somebody else's.

8/10/03

Columnist Tries to Avoid Controversy

This week I thought I would try to write about something non-controversial. So religion is definitely out. And the Bible. And politics – that knocks that in the head. Anything having anything to do with sex. In other words, all the really interesting stuff.

About all that leaves to write about is – you guessed it – salmon patties. Our topic for today is: "The Salmon Patty: Friend or Foe?" OR "So You Want to Be A Salmon Patty."

Here's an interesting fact about salmon patties which may surprise you. I know it did me. And that is this: Not everybody eats salmon patties. Growing up in southeastern Kentucky, I naturally assumed that everybody ate salmon patties. And why wouldn't they? They're delicious! They're nutritious! They're cheap and easy to fix! They provide seafood to those of us in land-locked states, and fish when it's too cold to fish.

But when I began to meet people from different places, I found out. Why some of them people never even heard of a salmon patty! Didn't even know what one was!

I heard on the news one time that a certain company that produced canned salmon was going to quit making it. Canned salmon wasn't profitable, they said, because it was consumed only in certain parts of the South. I think I know which parts.

I have done extensive, exhaustive and somewhat

fattening research on this topic, which required my visiting salmon patty websites, consuming large quantities of salmon patties, and conducting informal interviews with experts in the field (Hey, Ida and Hazel!). So I feel qualified to reveal yet another shocking fact about the salmon patty, and that is this: people disagree, sometimes violently, about how to make them.

Some people believe in draining the liquid off. Others religiously leave it in. Some remove the bones and skin, while others feel this would be wrong, very very wrong. There are the Fryers, the Bakers, and the Broilers. There are the Cracker Crumb People, the Bread Crumb People, the Corn Meal People, and the Flour People. There are Rice People, Cereal People and Mashed Potato People. There are those whose salmon orientation is toward "croquettes," while others prefer the more masculine term "salmon burger." And they put everything in there from coriander to coconut.

The sheer diversity of the salmon patty is a beautiful and mysterious and endlessly fascinating thing. But some people don't see it like that. They insist their way is the only way, and everybody ought to do like them.

They claim that they and they alone know what is good and right and true. But really they just know what they believe, what they like, what they're used to, and what they've always heard.

Next week: "Potato Salad and You."

10/20/03

Life Gets Teges

FINDING THE MUNDANE IN THE EVERYDAY

How Teges Got Its Name

A **lot of people** ask me where Teges got its name.

Okay. Almost nobody asks me that. But I tell them anyway.

Teges, as about everybody around here knows, was the nickname of local pioneer Adoniram Allen, who was so particular – or did they say peculiar? – that he got the name of being a very tedious fellow to be around.

Well, if you were a hundred and four years old, you might be tedious, too. Maybe Old Adoniram was one of these people that have to have things a certain way. Or maybe he just lived so long everybody got tired of him. I don't know.

Anyway, "Tedious" was pronounced "Tee-jus" and spelled "Teges."

So when a gas well blew up on Teges in the 1980s, the news man out of Lexington said it happened at a place called "Tay-guss." The way he said it, I didn't know where he was talking about, till I looked out the back door and the creek was afire.

There are actually two Teges Creeks, Upper and Lower, like teeth. They run into the South Fork of the Kentucky River about a mile or two apart from one another.

There used to be a post office at Teges, on the road between the mouths of the two creeks. I read that it was established in 1881 and that the first postmaster was Levi Abner.

I don't remember that far back, but I do remember the little post office and its last postmaster, Mae Webb Roberts, who for years wrote the "Teges Tips" for *The Manchester Enterprise.*

According to Robert Rennick's *Kentucky Place Names,* a lot of Clay County names go back to pioneer days. Hector, they say, is named for a dog that belonged to Abijah Gilbert, the first white settler up Red Bird.

Hector got killed by a bear on the creek bank, and Abijah thought so much of Hector, he named the creek after him.

Redbird, of course, was named for the Cherokee chief. The legend says that Red Bird and his companion Jack, sometimes called Crippled Jack, would come through here on hunting trips.

On one trip Red Bird and Jack were taking a nap at the mouth of Hector when a party of white hunters came through. The local people knew Red Bird and Jack and got along with them well. But this party of strangers included a man whose father had been killed by Indians.

Having vowed to take his revenge on any Indian he could, he slipped up on Red Bird and Jack, murdered them in their sleep with their own tomahawks, and threw their bodies in the river. Some of the local people retrieved the bodies and buried them. So the Red Bird River is named for the Cherokee chief, and Jack's Creek, they say, for his friend.

Another Clay County pioneer is said to have had three big hemlock trees in his front yard. In hot weather people going up and down Goose Creek would stop and rest in the shade of those trees.

The pioneer's name was Bright Short, and people got to calling that place "Bright's Shade." Brightshade.

Other places got their names later, when a little post office would be established and the first postmaster would have to turn in a name for it.

Sometimes they'd name them for themselves or somebody in their family. Like Bernice, Tanksley or Cottongim. The postmaster at Trixie named his for his dog. Sometimes, like at Garrard, Grace, and Sextons Creek, a community took the name of a local person or family.

A few places got their names from some prominent physical feature: Big Creek, Fall Rock, Mill Pond, Blue Hole, Burning Springs. Others, like Wildcat, Bar Creek, and Pigeonroost, were probably named for an animal found in abundance at that place.

Goose Rock and Goose Creek, some claim, were named for a goose that built her nest and raised her young on a rocky bluff above the creek.

There are two or three different stories about how Fogertown and Oneida got their names.

Fogertown might have been named for an old man who lived around there who used to ride up and down the road puffing on a big old pipe and fogging up the place. They got to calling him "Old Fogger," so when they needed a name for the town they just called it Fogertown.

Or it might have been named for an old woman who had big unruly white hair that looked like a fog had settled around her head. Or maybe it was just foggy around in there.

Oneida is the name of a Native American tribe, but nobody seems to know why our little town is named that. Some people think the town was named after the school, Oneida Institute. They say that James Anderson Burns, its founder, named the school after Oneida, New York, where a woman lived who donated a big lot of money.

Other people argue that the town was named first, and the school after that. Nobody seems to know for sure, and nobody knows for sure why around here we say "Oh – NEE - duh" when everybody else says "Oh – NYE - duh." Maybe they just thought "Oh–NYE–duh" sounded too proper.

Actually the old people called it "Oh–needy." So

I think it got its name because the people were so poor they were always hollering "Oh, needy!" Okay, I made that one up.

Road Run allegedly got its name from an old woman named Rhody who lived up there, who for some reason that I don't know and don't much want to think about, had to run pretty often to the toilet.

"Run, Rhody, run!" her husband would holler.

I don't know how historically accurate some of these stories are. To me it doesn't much matter.

Because whether they're fact, fiction or, like most stories, a little bit of both, they're part of our inheritance, along with the quilts, churns, homemade ax handles and other treasures our ancestors have handed down to us to keep.

We ought to keep the stories, too, and pass them on down to our children and grandchildren, the way the people did way back, when Hector was a pup.

11/1/01

The Creek and the Computer

Well, I'm about like Dewey Fox.

Before we got the cable down in here, we just got two channels on the TV, Channel 6 and Channel 10, both out of Knoxville. You couldn't really see Channel 10 very well, but we said we got it anyway, just so we'd have some variety.

Then they come out with the satellite dishes. Dewey didn't get a satellite dish, but Fanny and Woodrow got one, and Dewey went up and watched TV with them one time. I thought he summed it up about right. "There's ever quare thing in the world on there," he said.

Now we've got the Internet, and there's ever quare thing in the world on it, too. So it's a good thing you don't have to look at everything on there, but just what you want to look at.

But here lately some of the quare things have been coming over my computer whether I wanted them to or not, in the form of a virus. They call it a virus because it spreads fast and makes you feel miserable. The difference between a human virus and a computer virus is that somebody gives you the computer virus just for pure meanness.

My computer got a virus that made it start showing pictures of naked women. And I had not done a thing in the world to cause this to happen. No, really, I hadn't. But there they were in all their glory. I was outraged but more than that I was disinterested.

I deleted them off my computer, but before you could say Jack Robinson it had already sent them to everybody in my e-mail address book, including the preacher.

And that's not the only thing it's done.

It tries to boss. It won't even let me write like I want to. Ever time I go to write in good old hillbilly language, it tries to make me change it. It says some of the words I write are not real words. Well, I've been listening to words and using them about all my life and I think I know more about what a word is than some smart-aleck invention.

Sometimes it talks bad to me, accuses me of making fatal errors, performing illegal operations, first one thing, then another, and me not hurting a soul, just setting there trying to type, and never operated on anybody in my life. I'm about afraid it might call the law on me, for it can use the telephone by itself, don't think it can't.

Sometimes it warns me that if I keep on like I'm doing, it might become unstable. Well, Lord knows I don't want that. I've been through that before with people that became unstable, and I sure don't want to have to go through it with a computer.

Sometimes it stubs up and won't do a thing, won't even turn off. You have to jerk the plug out of the wall to get it to quit, then when you go to turn it on again it's mad because you didn't shut it down right.

I probably shouldn't own a computer, to tell you the truth. I'm no good at fixing anything like that. I don't even like to set the time on my digital clock. It works on my nerves. I'll fool with a song or a story, a sick pup or a pot of soup all day, but when it comes to a computer that's not acting right I have to take a nerve pill and call the neighbor's children to come and fix it.

I've thought about throwing it over the hill or in the creek any number of times, and I would, too, but for the environment. It's bad enough to have to look at all the old bedsprings and pop cans all over the place. I sure don't want to add a computer to the mess.

But if it starts in on me again, accusing me of things I didn't do and having bad talk and sending porno to the preacher, I'll get the gun, I swear I will, and I'll do the computer like Elvis did the TV. For I'll not put up with such as that in my own house now. I'll not.

1/31/02

Satellite Dish

W*ell, we finally broke down* and got a satellite dish. I'd been resisting it for years, for several reasons.

One, I thought the satellite dish would be about as big as our house, and I was afraid some photographers from off would come and take a picture of our little old hillbilly house beside our great big shiny satellite dish and put it on the cover of something with the caption, "Typical Appalachian home."

But the satellite man assured me that satellite dishes have got quite a bit smaller over the years, and sure enough, this one was about the size of a plate, and we hid it behind a bush in the yard so when the photographers come by they won't be able to see it.

So, on that point, it turned out I was wrong about the satellite dish.

Two, I thought you couldn't get local channels on a satellite dish, and I wanted to know what was going on in Kentucky, not just in California and New York.

But they said now you CAN get local channels on satellite, which, it turns out, is true to a point, but not entirely. We get the Lexington channels, but we can't get Hazard anymore, and I miss that. When you're talking about local, Hazard is a lot more local than Lexington is. On the Lexington stations, they think rain is a bad thing, because they can't go out and play golf. At Hazard, they understand that some people want rain for their gardens, and that we're not all big golfers.

And the weather channel has forgot where we live. When we had cable, the weather channel did not know where we lived exactly, but it had an idea we were somewhere between Corbin and Jackson. Now the TV has no earthly idea where we live and does not care. It tells us the weather for Atlanta and Boston and so on, or for the South and the Midwest, and since Kentucky falls in between the cracks on the weather map, we usually get left out altogether, unless we can come up with a good tornado or a flood or something.

So on the local channel issue, I was partly wrong about that, but partly right, too.

Three, when we had cable, I liked to go around and around and up and down the numbers looking for something interesting to watch. I was afraid if we got satellite, there'd be so many stations to look at, I'd wear myself out pushing the buttons and still wouldn't find anything good. And it turns out that on this point, I was completely correct.

My husband said if we got a satellite dish instead of cable, we would get a lot more channels for a little less money. And he was right about that. What he neglected to mention was that all the new channels we'd get would be just as stupid and boring and offensive as the ones we already got. There'd just be more of them.

"It's all Jesus and jewelry," somebody said, and at the end of both programs you can be sure they are going to want you to write them a check.

One good thing about it though, the picture's clearer. And since it takes too long to flip around the channels, I almost never come across the FOX so-called "News." And that is a good thing, for when I would accidentally stumble onto it before, it would always make me so mad I'd have to go out on the porch and holler real loud, and that would set all the dogs to howling and barking, and nobody on Teges could sleep a wink all night.

4/4/05

How to Get Dogs

"WHERE *did you get* all these DOGS?" people ask me as, knee-deep in a sea of mangy mixed-breed mutts, they struggle to make their way from their vehicle to my front door.

"It was easy!" I yell, trying to be heard above all the barking.

I suspect it's a rhetorical question. Most of my visitors aren't really that curious about the methods by which I acquired this menagerie. What they really mean is not "Where in the world did you get all these dogs?" but "WHY in the world did you get all these dogs?"

I can answer both questions.

It's easy to get dogs. All you have to do is nothing, and they will come to you. You will find them one morning under your car or on your back porch or lurking shyly at the edge of the yard, wondering if it's safe to come closer.

All you have to do to get dogs is, when they show up, don't shoot them. Don't throw rocks at them. Don't stomp your foot and holler "Git!" Speak to them in a soothing voice. Pet them if they'll let you. Give them food and water and an old shirt to sleep on, and they're yours for life.

That's a good way to get dogs, and I highly recommend it. It's very satisfying somehow to take a skinny, scruffy, scared little animal and watch it grow sleek and healthy, trusting and playful. Most dogs are gentle, and they don't really ask that much. They are, after all, God's creatures, and we are in some way responsible for them.

(There's another way to get dogs, of course, but I do not recommend it. If you don't get them spayed or neutered, every six months they'll multiply by seven or more.)

One reason I have so many dogs is just to try to do my part in the world, to lessen a bit the sum total of its misery. But I have other reasons, too, all of them selfish.

Every dog I have ever taken care of has paid me back a thousand times, in love, loyalty, gratitude, and just plain fun.

When I feel mad, sad, or otherwise tore up, I go and pet a dog. I stroke their soft warm fur. I tug gently at the scruff of their neck. I scratch around their ears. I rub the flat bony top of their heads. Pretty soon I feel a lot better.

I know some things they don't know, like algebra, a little French, and how to use the can opener. But every day, they teach me about patience, forgiveness and *joie de vivre*. They remind me that sometimes it's all right to just be.

Dogs aren't just a bother. They're a loud and reliable security system. They're good company. And easy to get.

9/26/02

How to Keep Dogs

So *we got* all these dogs. Mostly by just not running them off when they showed up. And people would give us dogs, often anonymously. And sometimes we'd forget to get the dogs fixed before they began to beget and begat, and so we got a lot more like that. (*See above,* "How to Get Dogs.")

So then we had dogs all over the place. Dogs in the front yard, dogs in the back. Dogs on the porch, dogs up in under the porch. And some dogs, not the brightest, out sunning themselves in the road.

And then they began to roam the countryside, frightening children and old people and terrorizing the neighbors' cats. And so, after a friendly visit from W.O. Henson, County Animal Control Officer, we decided we'd have to confine the dogs in some way.

Well, this was about Thanksgiving. And so we decided, rather than to purchase expensive Christmas presents for friends and family members, that we would instead purchase for each one a section of chain link fencing and put it up in their name and honor. So that's what we done and hit was a chain link Christmas.

Well, the dogs seemed pretty well satisfied inside their new chain link fence, and we were well pleased also. Grass began to sprout in the yard again. There wasn't so many gnawed-on old boots and beer cans drug in and strewed all over. You could go to the mailbox without being accompanied by a big rowdy pack of dogs.

114

The neighbors' cats could once again live their lives free from fear. And so everybody was happy, including W.O. Henson.

Well, that would have been a good ending to the story but that weren't the end of it. After months of confinement, all them dogs for some unknown reason up and decided all at the very same time that they wouldn't stay in the pen anymore, and they began to break out by a variety of means. Some figured out they could jump the fence. Some discovered they could dig their way out. While others, again, not the brightest, chewed their way through the metal gate.

So every day they'd get out and we'd put 'em back in and they'd get out and we'd put 'em back in and they'd get out and so on. And we hauled big rocks and big logs and threw in the holes the dogs had dug under the fence and we poured concrete and tried to fix the gate back where they'd chewed a big hole out of it. And they still got out.

So that's when we started talking seriously about electrifying the fence. And they must have heard us because now they've decided to stay in there. For the time being anyhow.

8/18/03

Old Sayings and New Appliances

My mother had these sayings.

"Too much is no better than just enough," she said. "If you can read you can do anything," she said. "Women must suffer to be beautiful," she said.

And after she got a dishwasher: "If it tears up, I'm buying a new one the same day," she said.

I've been thinking about that lately. I'm wanting to get me a dishwasher. They just cost about $300. I can afford that.

The trouble is, I don't have anywhere to put a dishwasher. When my ancestors built our kitchen, they did not foresee the invention of the dishwasher. Unfortunately they didn't foresee indoor plumbing, either, and they built the kitchen really low to the ground. An emaciated plumber plumbed it once a long time ago, and ever since then we've had to take a chain saw to the kitchen floor to get to the gas and water lines. I'm not kidding.

So a few years ago, I had a log room built on for a future kitchen. We've been using it for a dining room, but if I'm going to get a dishwasher, it makes sense to put it in there, where I've got the space, the wiring and the plumbing.

So now I need kitchen cabinets. But I can't find any that would look right in a 150-year-old house with a log kitchen built on. I'm having them hand made.

And clearly I cannot put my crummy old stove

and refrigerator in the same room with handmade cabinets and a new dishwasher. They'll have to be replaced.

And what about the freezer? There's nowhere to put it in the new kitchen, and I can't leave it in the old kitchen. That'll have to be our dining room, after we put the new floor in there (see "chain saw" *above*).

If I enclosed the deck and turned it into a utility porch, I could put the freezer out there. But then I'd have one of those situations where you have to go outside to get from one room of the house to another. To prevent that, I'll have to convert an existing window into a door and a door into a window.

Then I won't have a deck anymore, and I do so enjoy my deck, I'll have to build a new one the same day. The only place for a new deck is where the old smokehouse sets. I love the old smokehouse, which is an outstanding example of smokehouse architecture. The only way I could stand to see it torn down would be to have it reconstructed board by board in another location, and all this is starting to seem like a big lot of trouble to go to, just to keep from washing dishes.

Somewhere I've crossed the line from just enough over into too much. Or I need to read a good book on kitchen renovation. Or women must suffer to have dishwashers.

11/17/03

The Long Haul

My husband had a meeting at the Land Between the Lakes in western Kentucky, and I went with him. Then I had a meeting in Louisville, and he drove me up there. So in the course of one long weekend, we were in the car together for about twenty-one hours.

Our topic for today, boys and girls, is "The Difference between Men and Women."

Contrary to what you may have heard or imagined, the main difference between men and women is that, when starting on a trip, he will want to leave the house a lot earlier than is actually necessary.

She, on the other hand, will think it more important to look nice and to leave things in order than to adhere to some rigid, predetermined schedule.

He will want to drive fast and go straight there. This is because he knows that when he gets there, he is going to have to compare his performance with that of the other males in the areas of travel time, route planning and miles to the gallon.

She will want to stop at antique shops, outlet malls, and every bathroom between Pikeville and Paducah. She will place frequent and heavy demands on the vehicle's heating and air-conditioning systems.

She likes to roll the windows down in good weather, to feel the wind on her face. He prefers things like car windows and emotions to be sealed up tight.

She's in the mood for something they never eat at home, something involving walnuts, perhaps, or a raspberry vinaigrette. He's on the lookout for pie and potatoes.

At home he purports to suffer from a hearing disorder which prevents him from understanding and remembering a lot of what she says. In the car, however, his hearing becomes acute, his sensitive ears finely attuned to the most subtle variations in engine sounds. "Listen," he says, his head cocked to the side, his voice full of concern. "Do you hear that knocking (or clicking or whirring or whining or rattling) noise?" She doesn't hear it.

He points out things he thinks she might not notice, such as mountains, lakes, cities and weather. He says things like, "Who opened the gate?" and "They do a big business there," things which cause her to close her eyes and pretend to be asleep.

Despite these and other differences, my husband and I made it back home from our trip, still married, and without anybody even once cussing or crying or threatening to get out of the car and walk. This is probably due to me being such a saint.

Or maybe to the fact that, after logging thirty years and a lot of miles together, we try to laugh about our differences instead of arguing about them. We've settled down – for the long haul.

10/24/02

Who, What, When, Where, Why – and What?

Losing your memory. That's an amusing topic. Let's write about that. Okay, what was I saying?

I feel sorry for my husband because he is getting on in years and is losing his mind. Sometimes his train of thought jumps the track and goes crashing into a completely different subject.

He's got a good head for sports statistics, his job, and World War II, but certain other things he just can't seem to remember, like where we are going when we start out in the car, the gallon of milk he was supposed to pick up, or about that time he promised he'd do anything to make me happy.

I, on the other hand, remember that night quite well. This is because women have so many more brain cells than men to start out with. I can't remember where I read this, but we all know it's the truth. Otherwise, why would they have to keep asking us where the heating pad is?

In addition, the brain cells of women do not die off at nearly so rapid a rate as men's brain cells, which tend to get into fights with other brain cells, or get killed while attempting dangerous stunts, or simply atrophy and die from lack of use.

There are just a few things that I have trouble remembering. Unfortunately, one of them is other people. Like when you know you know somebody, but you can't recollect their name or anything about them. "How ARE you?" they ask. "GREAT!" you reply. And you have no more notion who that is than the man in the moon.

I have little tricks I use to help me remember certain things, like those pesky days of the week. Staring at a calendar is no help, since you have to have some information going in. Hearing the garbage truck is a clue. Or you can call and ask what the special is at Patty's. This will help you figure out the *when*, which frees you up to work on the *where*.

Say you're driving down a road you've been on a million times. And all of a sudden you don't recognize a thing. You panic for a second, thinking you've somehow fallen out of Tanksley into the Twilight Zone. Then it comes rushing back. Oh yeah, I know where I am.

Sometimes you know *where* you are but you can't for the life of you figure out *why*. You find yourself walking briskly and purposefully into a room. Then you pull up short. *What* am I doing here?

And so, in conclusion, we should all stop littering. You may need to consult a professional hairdresser. Art and religion. A better world. Stirring frequently until it's too late.

2/17/03

A Hot Topic

Much of the summer of 1962 I spent with my Aunt Mildred, a lovely woman, my father's sister, who lived at Gray Hawk in Jackson County. I was thirteen that summer. Mildred would have been forty-six.

I remember that in the middle of baking biscuits, stringing beans, digging for fishing worms or whatever else she was doing that summer, Mildred would suddenly stop and declare, "I'm having a hot flash!"

Then you had better get out of the way, for she would throw down whatever she had in her hand at the moment, and in a blur of dress-tail, apron-strings and house slippers, head at a dead run for the front porch, where she'd sit fanning furiously till the flash had passed.

There'd usually be a half dozen or more of us kids around Mildred's, and we all thought these hot flash episodes were pretty funny. Now, forty years later, I know what she was talking about.

It's hard to describe a hot flash, because happily there's nothing else like that. Imagine yourself popped like a tater tot into an oven preheated to 475 degrees. All of a sudden you're hot as a tater. You're hot as a griddle. You're hot as a red-hot poker. You're hot as, well, you-know-what.

For some reason when the hot flash flashes, you can't sit still. You're in the hot seat. You're on a hot rock. You've got to hot-foot it to a spot that's not so hot.

If you're cooking at the time, you can't stand the heat and you have to get out of the kitchen.

Then again, when you're hot you're hot, and when you're not you're not. You don't hear as much about it, but women in their mature years can get very cold also. Basically your thermostat's shot and anything can happen. Quick as a hot flash, your core temperature plunges. You're freezing and you can't get warm. You make hot tea and stoke up the fire. You pile on sweaters, housecoats, blankets and quilts.

Two minutes later, things start to heat up again, and you have to throw all that crap off, open the windows and turn the fans on high. It keeps a person busy just trying to regulate her temperature.

This next part may be too hot to handle, but ironically all this heating up occurs at a time in life when you're not really in the heat of passion anymore, let alone in heat. You're hot, but not the way you were before. You used to be a hot Mama. Now you're a hot Mamaw.

So listen, Hot Shot. If you drive by my house some frosty morning and see me outside in a pair of hot pants, drinking iced tea and fanning myself, just wave and drive on by. For some of us, it's going to be a long hot winter.

11/18/02

Breakin' Up Winter

I *live out in the country,* as a friend of mine
says, five miles from white bread, twenty-five from
wheat, fifty from rye and pumpernickel.

I remember, the first fall I lived out here, talking
with a neighbor about the oncoming winter. He dreaded
it, he said.

Why? I asked him. I'd always sort of liked winter.

So many things can go wrong, he said.

Since then I've had several chances to find out
what he meant. Pipes can burst. The well house can
freeze over. Ice can build up in the gas line.

But that's not the worst of it. If you've ever been
snowed in out in the country for a week or two, you
know what I'm talking about. Things can get weird.

You start to let yourself go. There's no use
brushing your teeth if you're not going to see anybody.
There's no use cleaning up the house if you're going to
be tromping in and out all day in muddy boots.

You begin to put together some very odd outfits,
like a long flannel gown accessorized by a hooded sweat
jacket, hunting socks and leopard-skin house shoes.
Dry air and static electricity make your hair whoof out
like a dandelion head.

Your only diversion is going outside to break the
ice on the dog's water. Cold seeps in through the cracks
in your psyche.

I don't know how long I'd been out here in this

124

shape. It seemed like six months or a year, but it might have just been since Christmas. I'd lost all track of time.

Finally I told my husband that if we did not go somewhere, and I did not mean Wal-Mart, that I was going to have to shoot myself or him one, I had not yet made my mind up which.

So that's how come us to go to Lexington a-Saturday.

And, honey, I had me a spree. I saw people that I did not know from Adam's off ox and they didn't know a thing about me. I could have told them anything and they'd have believed it.

I heard people speaking all kinds of different languages, Spanish, Japanese, I don't know what all. I ate things that I could not even pronounce, tasty dishes brought to me by attractive, attentive, obedient young men. Another basket of sourdough bread, please. And can I see the dessert menu?

I didn't do a thing all day that required me to have to put on coveralls, deal with a dead animal in any way, or even get out the toolbox.

And I bought an outfit so flamboyant that when I wore it to church the next morning, one of the elders said, "Sister Anne, what in the world have you got on?"

And so I was satisfied and thought the trip a great success.

1/27/03

City Water Comes to the Country

*T**his morning** they're laying the water lines along the road in front of our house.

I tear up my "To Do" list and go watch from the porch like a boy, mesmerized by the giant yellow machines scooping earth, the men holding back traffic with one hand, the steady roar of motors filling the valley.

We've been waiting for this for a long time.

When my great-grandparents bought this place in 1905, it had a dug well, which survived into the 1950s. I remember it as a storybook affair, six feet across, with moss-covered rock walls and a round wooden lid. A long rope lay draped in lazy coils on the side the well, tied to a battered metal bucket.

If you leaned over and hollered or sang down into the well, echoes came ringing back to you. When the light was right, you could see a reflection of your face, white and wavy on that dark watery mirror.

If the grownups weren't looking, you could throw rocks and other objects down in the well, and hear the thunk and watch the ripples when they hit. The cold sweet water, drunk from a dipper or a hollowed-out gourd, tasted of rain and moss.

The well offered, too, the thrill of danger. You might possibly fall in the well and drown, as other care-less and silly girls had done before, and that would be an end of you, since you had no Lassie to go for help, and no Trigger to pull you out.

The well opened into magic and mystery – a deep subject. Jesus met a woman at a well, and people in stories were forever meeting strangers at wells who turned out to be angels or witches. (Note: If somebody at a well asks you for a drink of water, give it to them.)

But the well we used more often was a less romantic drilled well, six inches across instead of six feet, lined with smooth metal. I liked watching my grandmother draw water from this well, liked how the muscles in her arms showed as she pulled up the heavy cylinder, hand over hand on the chain, liked how the water whooshed into the bucket when she pulled the metal ring.

I never thought about how often my grandparents had to do this, or about how hard a job it was. I don't remember their ever complaining about it. And I don't recall their objecting, either, when we got the electric well pump and indoor plumbing.

Like computers and other modern inventions, the new system made things easier when it worked, and harder when it didn't. The water tasted a little less like rain and moss, a little more like rubber and metal.

Over time, the quality of the water seemed to deteriorate. Gas wells leaked gas and oil into the water wells. Logging and mining operations filled the creeks with sediment. Straight pipes, inefficient septic systems, and other pollutants took their toll.

And the water had so much sulfur in it, our clothes, our sinks and tubs, even our teeth, turned a hideous shade of orange.

By the time my husband and I moved to the homeplace, the neighbors were taking their clothes to the laundromat in Manchester, and collecting their drinking water in plastic jugs at the spring in Oneida, where it drips off the mountain, clean and clear in all weathers.

We've been petitioning for city water here for years, and it looks like we're finally going to get it. It'll be good to be able to wash our clothes at home, and not to have to haul big bags of salt for the water filter, and not to have to worry about the pump going out or the well going dry or the water making us sick.

Once when I lived in Lexington, my uncle, who lived where I do now, came to see me. I got him a glass of water and took it to him out in the yard. "Thanks," he said, always polite, and took a big drink, which he immediately spat out on the ground. "Pew," he said, making a face. "City water."

Maybe I'll hang on to those plastic jugs a while, for occasional trips to the spring at Oneida. The old people here call it an "everlasting spring." I hope they're right.

4/21/05

Quit Makin' Fun of the Way I Talk

"I went to Ohio for my health," one feller told me. "I had to have something to eat."

A lot of us have had to go to Ohio for our health at one time or another. My grandfather went and got a factory job just long enough to work out the price of a cast iron cook stove. My uncle taught school up there for years. Other relatives, friends and neighbors have gone and stayed a lifetime.

Me, I didn't stay nearly that long. I just went and worked one day, visiting an elementary school in Cincinnati to talk about books and writing.

And I'm sure glad I didn't have to stay no longer than that. For I hadn't no more than got across the river before they begin making fun of the way I talk.

Now some people act like they don't mind it when people talk about their Kentucky accent. But I'm not like that. Hit makes me mad as far, and I'll tell you why.

Four main reasons. One, it's stupid. Two, it's ignorant. Three, it's snotty. And four, it's just plain rude.

(1) Stupid. It'd be pretty stupid to go up to somebody from England and say, "I notice you have an English accent." Or to say to a person from Mexico, "You talk like you're from Mexico."

Well, it's just as stupid to point out to somebody

from Kentucky that they talk like they're from Kentucky. Most of us have been told this a thousand times already, and probably don't need to have it pointed out again.

And it's just as offensive to tell somebody from Kentucky that they DON'T talk like they're from Kentucky. It suggests that they're either a big fat phony, or that it's a good thing they don't sound like they're from where they're from.

(2) Ignorant. Telling Kentuckians they have an accent is not only stupid, it's ignorant. It implies that Kentuckians have accents while other people don't. But people who study languages and dialects tell us that everybody has an accent. People from Kentucky have Kentucky accents. People from Ohio have Ohio accents. People from Wisconsin have Wisconsin accents. People on TV have TV accents. None of these accents is any better than any other. They're just different.

(3) Snotty. People who make this type of remark usually say it as if an accent were a bad thing to have, sort of like a disease. This is part of the condescending negative stereotypes many people hold about Kentucky in general and about Eastern Kentucky in particular.

Once somebody comments on your Kentucky accent, it's usually not long till they're inquiring whether you own a pair of shoes or have sex with close family members. One man in Ohio asked me if I ate possum much. I about choked on my pasta salad.

And it's not much better to comment on a person's accent and then claim that you like it. It's just the other side of the stereotype coin, the side where you're expected to play the dulcimer, sing big long ballads, and grow all your own food. Some people have actually ordered me to "say something. I love the way you talk." If I said what I was really thinking right then, they might not like it so well.

(4) Just Plain Rude. Even if you mean it as a compliment, commenting on somebody else's accent makes the person feel self-conscious and different. It distracts from the topic of the conversation, and makes the person feel as if you weren't really listening to what they said, only to how they said it.

How a person speaks is a part of who they are, an expression of their unique individuality and of the family and culture in which they grew up. The fact that we all speak somewhat differently from one another is interesting, but it's generally not good manners to comment on it.

5/2/02

Why I Hate Hillbilly Plays

*T*he minute you walk in the door, you can pretty well guess what you're in for. You've seen it a thousand times. Or maybe it just seems like a thousand.

The stage directions probably read something like this:

Curtain opens on backdrop of mountain cabin. On porch, two rocking chairs, a rickety table, a barrel, a brown drinking jug with three X's. In yard to left of cabin, a moonshine still can be seen.

Enter Maw. She is wearing a print dress, long apron, lace-up leather shoes, and heavy stockings rolled down around her ankles. Her white hair is pulled back in a bun. She looks over her glasses, which rest halfway down her nose. She is bent over with age, yet surprisingly spry.

She delivers her first line loudly, in an exaggerated hillbilly accent.

MAW: "Paw! Paw! Whur the Sam Hill air ye? Git chee fool self over hyur rite now ur I'm a-fixin' tuh shoot chee with this hyur shotgun!"

Enter Paw. He is wearing bibbed overalls and a straw hat. He is barefoot, sports a long beard, and is chewing on a blade of straw.

PAW (loudly, in an exaggerated hillbilly accent):

"Shucks, Maw! Land o' Goshen! Cain't a feller git no shut-eye around hyur? Me and Junior was up all nite a-runnin' the still. I'm plumb tuckered out."

And so on. The plot varies, but you can be sure that a possum will be involved, and a frying pan, a lethargic hound dog, probably named Old Blue, and of course the side-splitting antics of Maw and Paw.

The audience will roar with laughter. Because everybody agrees: Those hillbillies sure are funny.

But who are these hilarious hillbillies everybody enjoys laughing at so much? Who is this joke really on?

Could it be on us? No, we don't much think so. We like to think we're smarter, more modern, more sophisticated than the characters in hillbilly plays.

Well, if these shows are not about us, who are they about?

Maybe they're about the hillbillies of the past. Our ancestors, in other words. Well, I don't know about your ancestors, but mine had a measure of dignity about them. They worked hard. They thought about things. They felt things. They had joys and sorrows and tragedies in their lives. They were real human beings, who bore little resemblance to the ridiculous and demeaning figures that stomp around the stage in a hillbilly play.

So if these plays are not about us, and they're not about our ancestors, who are they about?

Maybe they're about those other Appalachians. You know, the ones who are not as educated as we are, not as sophisticated, not as well off. Is that who we're laughing at?

I hope not, because if it is, these plays are not only silly, but cruel as well. Is this what we want to teach our children? To laugh at the poor, the undereducated? To ridicule their relatives who are not as fortunate? To make fun of their neighbors who are not as blessed?

Maybe we're not making fun of people from around here at all. Maybe we're laughing at hillbillies from other places.

Well, where exactly do these other hillbillies live? Perry County? Pike? West Virginia? Tennessee?

I don't think so. I've been to those places, and the people there don't resemble these comical cardboard characters any more than we do.

In fact, no real hillbillies, no matter where or when they lived, have ever borne more than a superficial resemblance to the hillbillies in a hillbilly show.

So who are these comical hillbillies?

Who they are, of course, are not real hillbillies at all, but "play hillbillies," part of the popular American stereotype of Appalachians that has been around in various forms since the middle of the nineteenth century.

Stereotypes are made out of exaggerations, generalizations, half-truths and downright lies. They may see some small part of the truth, but they close their eyes to the rest of it. And what little they do see, they do not understand.

Stereotypes don't look far enough to see the diversity within a group. They don't look long enough to see how many people in a group don't fit the stereotype.

And they don't look deeply enough at the people who, in some ways, do seem to fit the stereotype. They don't see their humanity, their complexity. They don't look at the historic and economic forces that have contributed to the seemingly stereotypical behavior.

We Americans have a lot of stereotypes about each other.

According to the stereotypes, Native Americans are savages, African-Americans are lazy, Polish-Americans are dumb, Irish-Americans are drunks, Italian-Americans are all in the mafia, and Jewish Americans are tightwads.

Lately we've added another vicious stereotype which says that all Arab-Americans are terrorists.

Appalachian-Americans, according to the stereotype, are poor, barefoot, ignorant, backward, lazy and not very bright. They talk funny, marry their sisters, and are always feuding and making moonshine.

Hillbilly plays, no matter who puts them on, no matter why they put them on, and no matter how funny they think they are, are based on negative and demeaning stereotypes of Appalachians, stereotypes that were created and perpetuated by people from outside the region for their own amusement and for the pleasure of feeling superior to us.

Surely with all the resources we have now, and with all the educated and talented people around, surely we can come up with better shows than this for our children to see and to participate in.

Because whether we admit it or not, this joke's on us, and we ought to quit helping them tell it.

11/8/01

Mules, Haints & Asphalt Salesmen

POOR,
BUT WE'VE GOT STORIES

Once Upon a Driveway

*T**he other morning*** I was setting drinking a cup of coffee when there come a knock-knock-knock at the door. And I said to myself, now who is it, the Big Bad Wolf?

So I went to the door and there was this feller, I never had seed him before. He'd been working down the road here, he said, and he had a little bit of asphalt left over. And did I want him to fill in at the end of our gravel driveway, there where the driveway meets the road?

Well, that needed doing, I knew. But I had heard before of people being took in and took advantage of and took for everything they had by unscrupulous person-ages going around the countryside, and I wanted this feller to know and realize just what a shrewd customer and sharp cookie was dealing with, and not somebody about to be took, in any shape form or fashion. So I just up and asked him, bold as you please, I said, how much would it cost?

A dollar a foot, he says. So I done some quick calculating there in my head and estimated, what I wanted done, hit would cost me about twenty-three dollars. So I said all right, go ahead then, and I went back in the house.

In a little while here he come back with a big gang of workmen. And oh what big trucks they had! And what big rollers and dozers they had! And oh what a big racket they made! And that's when I first begin to suspect this might cost more than twenty-three dollars.

After while here he come a-knock-knock-knocking again, and said they was done, for me to come and look. And lo and behold if they hadn't blacktopped about the whole dad-blame driveway. I expressed some of my feelings about it, which was a complex mixture of emotions. But the feller explained to me, that all that was, hit was just the extry asphalt that he had left over.

That was one thing about asphalt, he said. You couldn't get just a little bit of asphalt. If you were going to get any asphalt at all, you had to get a big lot. And you had to put it all down right then, he said, while it was good and hot. You couldn't wait.

Then I felt kindly embarrassed and low down, not to know any more about asphalt than I did. But he said not to worry about it, he'd just charge me the same. Which I took to mean, the same as if he hadn't of done all that. So then I took my little basket of goodies and skipped on down the path to grandma's house.

Well, after while here he come back up on the porch with his measuring wheel and his calculator and his pencil and paper. I reminded him how I had not requested to have my driveway blacktopped, and he said he'd knock a little off the bill, on account of me being so ignorant about asphalt. So he set there a while doing arithmetic, adding and subtracting and multiplying and dividing a sight, and then he said, well, at a dollar-fifty a square foot, altogether hit come to four thousand eight hundred and thirty-five dollars.

Well, I didn't know whether to laugh or cry. So I laughed. And I told him, which was the gospel truth, that I didn't have nowhere near that amount, had no way of getting it, and what's more if I did have it, I would probably not spend it on asphalt.

Well he huffed and he puffed and he said it was a bill and had to be paid. That was another thing about asphalt, he said. It had to be paid for the same day you got it. And he offered to take me to the bank right then so I could take out a loan. I was about to say something like, 'Not by the hair of my chinny chin chin,' when the telephone rang.

And it was not a hunter, but my husband. And I told him the whole story. I don't remember what he said exactly, but I know it had the word LAWYER in it, and the word SCAM, and something about CALLING THE SHERIFF.

So then I went and told the feller all what my husband had said. And almost like a miracle this feller was overcome with a spirit of generosity, and offered to give me the whole driveway free of charge.

No, I said, I'll pay ye for what I wanted done, and we settled up and he left. With his workmen and his rollers and dozers and trucks, all in somewhat of a hurry, it seemed to me.

So that's all the story. But remember. Watch out. For one day the Big Bad Wolf may come a-knock-knock-knocking at your door, too. The End.

9/1/03

❧

Storehouse of Memories

Lucy Baker's store went down the South Fork with the '47 flood, and she never did build it back after that. So my grandfather cut oaks and poplars off the hillside and built a store himself.

My grandparents Bradley and Carrie Bishop, and later my uncle Millard Bishop, ran that store for more than forty years. My husband and I tried to keep it going, but we couldn't make the math come out. Now you have to pay these big companies so much to haul stuff out here that nobody can afford to buy it. The storehouse still stands, but now it's filled with broken chairs, dusty old books, and memories.

It used to be quite lively. When I was a kid big crowds would gather on Sunday afternoons, to drink pop, chew tobacco, laugh and talk and tell big tales and just generally enjoy one another's company. Most of those people are gone now – Shade and Dewey Fox and their wives Marthy and Orthie, Morris and Till Allen, Eugene Allen, Woodrow and Fanny Baker, Mae and Malcolm Roberts, P.J. and Emma Baker, Fred Moore, George Felty, Ailie Felty, Dorie and Jess Robertson, Mary and Virgil Webb, Lucian Allen.

My grandparents opened the store for business evenings and weekends, but weekdays they generally kept it closed. Through the week people just popped in – one now and another one after while – so my grandparents didn't want to set at the store all day long and them with a big lot of work to do.

So they'd be at the house or the barn or in the garden or the field or the tobacco patch, and if you wanted in the store you'd have to stand with your hands cupped around your mouth like a megaphone and holler them out. "Whooooo Carrie! Whoooooooo Bradley! I'm a needin' in the STORE !!!"

Then one of them, usually Carrie, would come and open up the storehouse and you could get your pop or your plug of Hornet or your Betty Rose liniment or whatever it was you come after.

Virgil Webb told me a tale one time about something that happened at the store. He didn't swear right up and down it was the gospel truth. He just told it. So that's what I'll do, too.

Now Lucian Allen was a smart man and a good man, no doubt about it. Jess Wilson remembers Lucian devising a system of wires and pulleys to move tobacco down these steep hillsides from the patch to the barn.

Lucian did a big lot of carpenter work around in here, and a lot of his work we're still using today. He helped build the Road Run church house, and he helped my grandfather work on the house I live in now. One time they had the roof off the house and it commenced to rain in the night. They were all running around trying to cover stuff up, looked out and here come Lucian up the road from his house to help, in the rain and the dark with a lantern in his hand.

Virgil told it that one day Carrie and Brad were in the field hoeing corn when Lucian come and hollered them out. So Carrie laid down her hoe, pulled the store key out of her apron pocket and went to see what Lucian was a-wanting. Well, he was about dead with the bellyache, he said, and what did she think he ort to take for it?

"Well, I always take a Alky-Seltzer, Lucian," she told him, and handed him a bottle to take home with him. Well, right then a big rowdy gang come in from Ohio and begin purchasing beans and viennies and sardines and crackers and cigarettes and stick candy and I don't know what all, and Carrie got to waiting on them and forgot all about Lucian and his belly.

Well, Lucian, in the meantime, went and set on the bench out in front of the store and before anybody could stop him he'd opened the lid on that Alky-Seltzer, popped two big tablets in his mouth, chewed them up a little bit and swallered them.

Well, it werent' too long after that he come up off of that bench and commenced to run right backwards and forwards in the middle of the road, foaming at the mouth and carrying on till they always said hit was a thousand wonders somebody hadn't a come along and shot him.

Well, they seen pretty quick what the trouble was and somebody handed Lucian a pop to drink and he drunk that and seem like that made him a lot worser than he was before.

About that time Bradley come a running from the field to find out the cause of the commotion, then he went to the house and brought back a jar of well water for Lucian to drink and he drunk that. Right at first seem like he got worser again. Then he might have got a little bit better. Then he got a little bit more better and then he got all right.

After while some of them asked him, said, "Lucian, brother, how'd you like the Alky-Seltzer?"

Lucian shook his head and answered solemn, "I'll never take another'n."

8/22/02

Pea Pickin' Tale

It's pea pickin' time in Kentucky, and my buddy Winton Allen that lives down on Newfound told me a tale about stickin' peas when he was a boy on Teges. Here's Winton's story.

They was an elderly lady lived in Doc's cabin, just up and across the road from where we lived. Ailie Felty always wore a apron. She was a good lady.

She had a garden across the creek from her place, and she'd planted some early peas, garden peas. And she told me she says, Winton, if you'll cut the pea sticks and stick my peas for me, I'll give ye a penny for ever stick you cut and another penny a stick to stick the peas and get the vines started up 'em.

So I went to the woods and cut little sprouts to stick them with. It took a hundred sticks. I got it all done and Ailie was bragging about what a good job I did and what a good boy I was.

I got my two dollars – which was a big lot of money for a kid back then – and went to Brad and Carrie's store to get me some Bazooka bubble gum. You could get a girlfriend with Bazooka bubble gum. You'd give a girl a piece of that, she'd sorter pass you a note, and you'd call her your girl friend.

So – the peas was stuck, I got my money, I got my Bazooka, and I got me a girlfriend.

But they was another lady heard what a good job I done and wanted me to stick her peas too. I agreed. Well, rather than to go to the woods and cut another hundred sticks, I just went to Ailie's garden and pulled up the ones I'd cut for her.

I was about half done sticking peas in the second garden when George Felty and Shade Fox popped up and wanted to know where I'd got my pea sticks at. I told 'em, I even went and showed them where I'd cut 'em.

But when George Felty took me gently by the arm, I found out I was not as slick a fox as I thought I was. I got caught. And had to stick both patches again without pay.

But Ailie, bless her soul, she felt sorry for me and give me another dollar. Then the other lady said I done such a wonderful job she would pay me the same thing Ailie did, which was three dollars. So I ended up getting two extry dollars for doing wrong.

But alcohol was fifty cents a bottle, and it took two bottles to cure the welts on my legs. So that took one dollar off my profit.

And the other extry dollar, I put that one down to pain and suffering.

6/9/03

One Time There Was This Mule

*O**ne time there was this mule**,* and the feller
that had it, he kept his mule a long time after everybody
else had traded theirs in for a tractor. He still plowed
with his mule, and ever Sunday evening he hitched it up
to the old buggy and went for a ride.

Well, he was riding along behind his mule one
Sunday and here come a gang of boys barreling down
the road about ninety miles an hour in their daddy's old
pickup. The mule got skittish and dived in the ditch-
line head foremost – wagon, feller and all. Well, it like to
killed the mule, but the feller said he was all right.

But after a time seem like his back got to hurting,
and he decided he'd up and law the boys that was driving the truck.

So they all went before the judge. And the lawyer
for the boys, he put the feller on the stand that had the
mule. And he asked him, said, "Now sir, will you please
explain to this court how it is that at the time this inci-
dent occurred, you reported that you had sustained no
injuries whatsoever, and yet now you come before this
court claiming to be bad hurt."

The feller that had the mule said, "Well, since
you've asked me I'll tell ye. When I was a-laying in the
ditch-line, the sheriff come along. He looked at the
mule, seen it was hurt, pulled out his pistol and shot it
in the head. When he started over towards me, I hollered out loud as I could, 'I never felt better in my life!'"

Tennessee storyteller Doc McConnell told that tale last weekend at the National Storytelling Festival in Jonesborough. There were storytellers there from all over the country, several of them from Appalachia.

Elizabeth Ellis, one of the best-known and best-loved storytellers in the country, is originally from Owsley County. She's lived in Texas for many years, but you can still hear Kentucky in her voice.

Bill Lepp, who holds the dubious distinction of being a five-time winner of the West Virginia Liars' Contest, tells hilarious stories that are part personal experience, part tall tale.

Shelia Kay Adams sang songs and told stories from her home in the mountains of North Carolina. And some people will tell you that Donald Davis, also from Appalachian North Carolina, is the best storyteller in the country.

The festival was amazing, and I plan on going back every chance I get. But we don't have to go to a festival in Tennessee to hear good stories and good Appalachian storytellers. They're all around us. All we have to do is pay attention.

10/10/02

Poor, But We've Got Stories

We *might not have too much* around here
in the way of jobs, money, city water and so forth, but
we are well off in stories. It gives us something to talk
about while we work on our old well pumps and watch
the drug traffic go by.

We've got the Saddler Booger, whom you might
meet if you head up Saddler Branch late of a night. He
used to jump on the back of people's horses. Then he
took to catching rides on the running boards of their
cars. Now, they say, when you look in your rear-view
mirror, you're liable to see him in the back seat. Even a
booger has to keep up with the times.

And we've got the legend of Sally Railsplitter, who
could split rails as well as any man and made a good
living at it. People suspected she had a big lot of money
stashed somewhere but they didn't know where, and
then she up and died and they never did find it.

In the 1930s, when they were building the road
through here, blasting rock off the Crane Cliff, they
found, in a cave of a place on the side of that mountain,
an old mattress tick stuffed plumb full of money. Sally
Railsplitter's, they figured.

One of the men said he'd take it home with him
and find out who it legally belonged to. But you know
that feller disappeared after that, and so did the money.

And then we've got the one about the old man
and old woman that lived away up in the head of one of

these hollers. This was away back before there were any cars in this country, and the old man and woman, they never had been anywhere much and they never had seen a car, didn't even know what one was.

Well, one day a car come up the holler and pulled up right in front of their house. The old woman looked out the window and hollered, "Lord have mercy! They's a critter outside with a hard shell and two big white eyes, and hit's a-growling right low and mean!" And she dove in under the bed and hid.

The old man grabbed his shotgun and commenced to fire at the car. So the feller that was in there, to save his life, jumped out as quick as he could and run up in the woods.

The old woman come out from under the bed then and asked the old man, said, "Well, did you kill the critter?"

"I do not know," the old man said. "But I made it turn loose of that feller."

1/20/03

Witches, Haints & Hyenas

***T**hings just kept happening* to them. A cow would die, or a sow would have pigs and they would all die. So they went to see this old elderly man that was said to be a witch doctor.

He told them to go home, get a big fat hen, kill the hen, take the heart and stick ten new pins and ten new needles in it, and throw the heart in the fire while you cook the hen. Said it will jump out and holler quit but you pick it up and throw it back in the fireplace each time until it burns up. So they done that.

The witch doctor also told them said someone will come again and again and want to borrow something but said don't let them have anything. So sure enough a neighbor girl came and first wanted to borrow an iron and then a bucket and then some matches but was told no.

A few days later one of the neighbor men got real sick and died. When they went to lay him out, they saw on his chest the print of a heart with looked like pins and needles sticking out of it.

That story was sent in by Mae Henson of Oxford, Alabama, who was born on Little Sextons Creek in Clay County. She said her dad told it to her, and his grandparents had told it to him.

Richard Stamper of Campton, Kentucky, who

writes a column for the *Wolfe County News*, shared this next one, which he swears is the truth.

⋘

Well what happened, this feller was spending the night in the graveyard, just to show he could, to prove he weren't afraid of anything. And he was laying out on the ground asleep under some covers when he waked up and seen two big white eyes, down low to the ground, staring right straight at him.

Well naturally he took out his pistol and shot at them eyes. But sadly, as he found out right quick, they was his own two big toes, shining in the moonlight. And being a pretty fair shot, he had done and blowed one of 'em about plumb off.

⋘

Junior Ray Hoskins wrote in and told it that when he was a youngun on Elk Creek, one night they heard the awfullest screams ever was, coming from under the floorboards of the house. His granddaddy shot the shotgun, and the thing that screamed, everwhat it was, come out from up in under the house and run up in the hill.

Some said it was a woman. Some said it was a fox. Others claimed it was a deformed hyena escaped from the Dogpatch Zoo.

But nobody never did know for sure.

5/12/03

Haint Tale

"There is only one haint tale**, and this is
it." That's what Richard Chase, collector of the Jack
tales, said about "The Haunted House."

There may be only one haint tale, but there are
many different versions of it. Leonard Roberts, who
collected folk tales in Eastern Kentucky in the 1940s
and '50s, said it was the tale he heard most often. My
version combines two versions Roberts collected, one in
Knox County and the other in Leslie.

The Haunted House

One time away back they was this family – a man,
a woman, and a little girl. They got put out of their
house so they were out on the road looking for somewhere to stay.

Well, they went along and towards dark they seen
a house didn't look like anybody lived in it. So they went
to the house across the creek to ask about it. And a
feller told them, no, didn't nobody live there. Different
people had tried to live there but couldn't. They all
complained it was haunted.

Well, they decided they'd stay there anyway, so
they went and fixed their beds and built a fire, and then
the man went back up the road to the store to buy them
something to eat. Well, he got to talking to some fellers
and didn't come back till away up in the night. So the
woman and the little girl were there by theirselves.

The woman put the little girl in the bed and then she went and set in front of the fire. After while she heard something upstairs, sounded like chains dragging across the floor. Looked and down the steps come a coffin, floating in mid-air.

The woman thought she might as well go and open the coffin as not. She lifted up the lid, and there laid a dead man, or what was left of one. And then she remembered what you are always supposed to say to a ghost if you see one.

"In the name of God, what do you want?"

"I thank you for asking," said the man in the coffin. "I've been trying to get somebody to talk to me for ten years but they always run off."

He said that was his house and he'd been killed for his money, but the robbers never found it. He said if she'd go get the law and bring them out there, he'd tell them who killed him. Then he wanted to be laid in the ground proper.

"If you'll do all that for me," he told her, "you can have this place and all my money. It's hid in under that hearth rock."

So the woman done all what the ghost told her to. And her and her man and their girl lived there and got along good. And the ghost rested easy.

10/31/02

154

The One About the Turtles

*U**sed to,* pack peddlers would come through this country on foot, selling candy, combs, needles and threads, just different little things like that, out of packs they carried on their backs.

Well, one time a peddler come through and was going from house to house up on Saddler, and he stopped to rest by the creek at a place where there weren't no houses. And a man that lived around in there come by. I don't know if they got into it over something or if it was just for pure meanness, but that man killed that peddler, held his head under water in the branch till he drowned. And nobody saw it but the turtles in the creek.

When they found the peddler's body, didn't nobody know where he come from nor who his people was nor nothing about him, so they just put him in the ground and never had much of a service for him.

Well, years passed and the man who murdered the peddler, he got old and died. And they was aiming to put on a big fancy funeral for him, because he was a big important man, well-known in the community. The night before the funeral they had him laid out at his house, and people come to set up all night with the corpse.

Away up in the night, they heard something out on the porch, and some of them went out there to see what it was. And all over the place, all over the porch and all up in the yard and coming all down the road as far as they could see, was turtles, hundreds and hundreds of turtles headed right straight towards that house.

The people started running around as quick as they could trying to close all the doors and winders, but they couldn't keep all the turtles out, and a big lot of turtles got in and headed right straight to the room where that man laid a corpse. And they climbed up in his coffin and begin to eat the flesh off his bones. All the other turtles waited outside in the yard and all over the place, so the people was afraid to try to leave from there.

When daylight come, all that was left in that coffin was a skeleton. Then all the turtles turned around and went back to wherever they come from.

To this day some people claim that if you're walking by yourself up Saddler, you can hear something walking behind you, and when you stop, it stops, and when you start again, it starts, too. Most people just hear it, but a few say they've seen it, too, walking forever up and down the Saddler Branch, with a pack on its back.

10/27/03

Old First

Some people collect stamps. Or coins or antique dishes. I collect stories.

Some of the best ones I learned from Jess Wilson of Possum Trot who, long before anybody else around here, knew the value of these homegrown tales.

One of my favorite Clay County stories is the story of Old First Davidson, which appears in Jess' book, *The Sugar Pond and the Fritter Tree.* Jess says he heard the story in 1957 from Mr. Roland Hunter (R.H.) Davidson at Brutus on Bullskin Creek.

I got the story from Jess, but like most storytellers, I seldom tell a story the way I heard it. Here's how I tell "Old First."

Well, this story come down through the Davidson line. It's about the first Davidson that was ever in this country.

I can't tell you just exactly when it was, but it was way back. So fur back we've forgot his Christian name. We always just call him Old First.

Now back in them days people didn't have all these radios and television sets and movies and what not. To entertain theirselves they'd sing, dance, play music, play games, pull pranks, or tell big tales, like I am now.

And some people would fight. Not because they

157

was mad necessarily, but just for the sport of it. Sort of like boxing or wrestling is now. Just fighting for the sport of it.

And Old First Davidson was the fightinest man, I reckon, when he was young, that was ever in this country. Big stout feller, with a chest like a barrel, shoulders like an ox, arms like tree trunks and hands as big as hams. Fit ever body he could get up with and whupped ever one.

So after while it got to where he couldn't find nobody to fight with. Well, to tell the truth, he was getting tired of it anyway. All that hair-pulling, teeth-breaking, nose-blooding and rib-cracking. Anything gets old. So Old First decided he'd give it up. Quit fighting, set on the porch, and try to live peaceable.

Well, it went along like that awhile. Then one day Old First was out on the porch, a-puffing on his pipe, when a stranger on a horse rode up to the gate.

"What can I do fur ye?" Old First asks him.

"I have come all the way up here from the state of Tennessee," says the stranger. "I'm trying to find a feller by the name of Old First Davidson. Do you know where I can locate him at?"

"You're looking right at him," says Old First.

The stranger claimed to be the fightinest man in the state of Tennessee. Said he'd whupped so many down there, he'd run out of people to fight with. He'd heard tell of Old First and had rode all the way up from Tennessee to fight him.

Old First studied on that a minute. Then he says, "Well, I reckon I'll fight ye if you want me to. But no use to get in a big hurry about it." Says, "Set down and rest a spell. We might as well eat a good meal before we fight. Hit's about ready, and the wife'll get mad if we let it get cold."

Tennessee tied his horse to the gatepost and stepped up on the porch.

About that time Mrs. Old First Davidson come out with a dish rag in her hand and said, "If you men set out here and let the dinner get cold, I'll throw it to the dog and whup ye both."

So they went in and eat dinner, and when they got done, they went back out on the porch.

Tennessee was chomping at the bit to fight. Old First eased back in his chair and lit his pipe. "I never do like to fight right after I've eat a big meal," says Old First.

"Looky here," says Tennessee. "I've come a long way to fight you now, and I won't be put off no longer. Come and fight or I'm calling ye a coward and a weakling."

Old First grinned, laid down his pipe, and slowly stood up. "Well, if you will be to fight," he says, "I reckon I'll have to fight ye. But first let's move some of this stuff out of the way. The wife'll get mad if we thrash around and tear up the place."

Well, even a stranger from Tennessee could see that Mrs. Old First Davidson wasn't somebody you wanted to make mad if you could keep from it. So he lit in helping Old First move stuff out of the yard to make a place to fight.

Old First got the flower pots out of the yard and set them up on the porch. Tennessee run the dog out of its house and hoisted the dog house up on the porch by the flower pots. There was a bench out under the big shade tree, and they packed that up on the porch, too.

Well, in the meantime, Tennessee's horse had got loose and wandered up in the yard a-picking grass. When Old First seen that, he didn't do a thing in this world but go and crouch down underneath that horse. Then he picked the horse up and set it over the fence, with no more trouble than if it'd a-been a cat. Never even got red in the face.

Tennessee's eyes got big as saucers.

Well, there was a big old rock in the yard, a boulder is what it was. Tall as one outhouse and wide across as two. Mrs. Old First had whitewashed the rock and planted posies around it. She thought the world of that rock.

"The wife'll get mad," says Old First, "if we bust up her rock."

Old First picked the rock up with one hand and set it over the fence with the other. Didn't even break a sweat.

Tennessee's eyes popped out on stems.

Tennessee stood there looking at Old First. Old First stood looking at the shade tree.

"That's a good shade tree," says Old First. "I shore would hate anything to happen to my shade tree."

Old First put his arms around the trunk of that tree, pulled it up by the roots, and set it gently over the fence. Didn't even grunt.

Well, I can't tell you what Tennessee's eyes done that time. For he took out of there so fast, all you could see was his shirttail a-flying.

He headed over the ridge and run, they said, all the way back to Tennessee. Never did come back for his horse.

Old First Davidson kept that horse and worked it. Treated it good.

And when it died, he kept the horseshoes and passed them down to his children. And they passed them down to their children and they passed them down to their children and they passed them down to their children. On like that.

Some people claim this story ain't the truth. But I have been right at the Davidson homeplace, and I have seen them horseshoes. They had them hanging up over their barn door a long time.

As far as I know, they're hanging there yet.

10/18/01

160

Woman at the Well

Once there were two sisters. One was kind, good, helpful and open-hearted, but the other was mean, lazy, stingy, selfish and not much account at all.

Well, one day they were at the house and the water bucket got empty. So their mother told the mean lazy sister to go to the well and draw a bucket. But the girl sassed her and said, no, she weren't about to, she was too good to go to the well and draw water. So the other one went, the one that was kind and good and so forth.

Well, she drew her bucket of water, turned around to head back to the house and there stood a real old woman, skinny, humped over, and dressed in the raggedyest outfit you ever saw in your life. And she asked that girl, said, "Honey, would you give me a little sip of water?"

The girl said she shore would, and she give the old woman a good cold drink of water. And then the old woman said, "Honey, you've been so good to a poor old woman, you're about to get a reward. From now on out, ever time you comb your hair you'll comb out pearls and diamonds."

The girl said, "Well, all right," and she took her water bucket and went back to the house, never thought no more about it.

Well, that night before she got in the bed she went to comb her hair, and pearls and diamonds commenced to fall out of it and roll all over the floor. And when her mother seen that she said to the no account girl, "I want you to look at what's come out of your sister's head." The kind-hearted girl said she believed it'd been like that ever since she'd went to the well that day. Then they got in the bed and went to sleep and slept all night.

Right early the next morning the no account sister got up and told her mother she was going to the well to see if she couldn't get her some jewels, too. She didn't much like her sister to have anything and her not have it.

So she went and was standing by the well when that same old woman come up and asked her for a drink of water. And that girl said, "No, I ain't a foolin' with you. I'm about to get me some pearls and diamonds." Told the old woman to go on and get away from there. "And get out of my face," she said.

The old woman disappeared and after while when nothing else happened the no account girl went on back to the house.

Well, she no more than stepped in the door till here come Mommy with a comb in her hand, said, "Set down and let me comb your head." So she set down. Her mother commenced to comb and out of that girl's hair leaped a hundred snakes and a thousand frogs. And they hopped and slithered all over the floor and got into everything in the house and there was not a thing in the world they could do about it.

So that was the end of that.

Our water bucket got empty the other day, too, and I had to go to the spring at Oneida to fill it up again. Only now we use plastic jugs. And I met a sweet and interesting woman there, two of them, in fact. We started trying to clean up the trash around the spring, and we got to talking while we did it. They told me a story about a woman who was buried alive somewhere up one of these hollers. If you go up in there, they said, you can hear her.

They asked me if I reckoned that story was the truth. No, I said. I don't believe in such as that. Probably just something people told to be telling something, or to scare little children so they wouldn't go off too far from the house.

But after the women left I got to thinking. Maybe there was something to that story. There have probably been women buried alive up all these hollers. Not under rocks and dirt, but under other weights – poverty, relentless physical labor, the demands of a domineering husband and a big gang of children.

In folklore and in the Bible, a well or a spring represents an intersection between the known and the unknown. They can be sources – "wellsprings" – of knowledge, power and renewal.

I collected my jugs of water and went back to the house, thinking about wellsprings, the people we meet at them, the lessons we learn, and about the woman up in the holler, buried alive.

3/21/02

Is This Your Story?

You got clumsy and fell down the back porch steps. You ran into the bathroom door in the dark. You tripped over one of the kids' toys and landed on the floor, face first.

At least that's what you tell people, when they ask you what happened, where you got that black eye and those bruises on your arm. And those are just the ones they can see.

You can tell by the way they look at you that they don't really believe your explanations anymore. They've heard these stories too many times. But they go on pretending, and so do you, that everything at your house is A-okay.

It's your secret, yours and his, and you're going to help him keep it, even if it means lying to your family, your friends, your kids, and most of all to yourself.

You're going to help him keep the secret because, for some reason that doesn't make any sense, even though he's the one who's acting ugly, you're the one who feels ashamed.

You're going to help him keep the secret because you think, you hope, you pray, that somehow the abuse will just stop, and things will get better again.

Maybe you feel sorry for him. His childhood wasn't so hot. He has trouble at work. The guys he hangs out with drink too much and are heavy into drugs. If he could just get off those, maybe he'd straighten up. Maybe he'd quit being so rough on you.

Maybe you still love him. He can be so sweet sometimes. He tells you he loves you. He cannot live without you. He'll kill himself if you leave him. He loves you too much, that's why he's so jealous. He doesn't want you to look at another man. He doesn't want you to talk to another man. He doesn't want you spending time with your family or your girl friends anymore. They don't like him, never have. They think he's not good enough for you. They don't understand the way you two feel about each other. It's really something special.

If you would just do exactly what he says and not make him so mad and not make him lose his temper, everything would be all right. Just do what he wants. Let him run the show. Let him handle the money. Dress like he wants. Act like he wants. Don't go anywhere he doesn't want you to go. Don't talk to anybody he doesn't want you to talk to.

He promises, if you'll try, he'll try. He's sorry, baby, really sorry. He will never do it again. Swear to God.

And so you try. You walk around on eggshells trying not to upset him. You try to remember all his little likes and dislikes. You try to please him. You try to read his moods.

But none of this works, because anytime, when you least expect it, out of a clear blue sky, he can blow up again. And you end up with a swollen face, a split lip, a broken rib, a broken heart, or worse. Some things he's said to you, some things he's done to you, you can't even stand to think about.

Maybe, deep down, you think you deserve this. You never did think much of yourself, not really. You think you're not as smart, not as good-looking, not as interesting as other people. He's put you down so much, with his insults and knocking you around, he's got you thinking you don't deserve any better than this.

You keep the secret for some or all of these reasons, but mostly you keep it because you're afraid of what he'll do to you if you tell. You've seen that look in his eye. He could kill you, and you know it.

It's hard to change your life when you're just trying to survive. It's hard, but it's not impossible. And you do deserve better than this. It's not your fault. It's his. And there's no excuse for it – not stress, not a bad childhood, not a hard day at work, not your human imperfections, not alcohol and drugs. There is no excuse. And it isn't going to just stop. It's probably going to get worse.

But you do have options. The law is on your side, if you will use it. And you are not alone. There are places you can get help.

This wasn't always the case. For a long time, law enforcement, the courts, and society as a whole tended to look the other way. A man's home was his castle, they said. What's between a man and his wife is private business, they said. Every couple has their little squabbles and spats, they said.

But now we have a better understanding of domestic violence. We know that getting beat up is not a squabble, and deliberate cruelty is not a spat.

We know that when it comes to domestic disputes, men and women are not on a level playing field. Some men are victims of abuse, but ninety-five percent of domestic violence victims are women. Every fifteen seconds in the United States, another woman gets beaten. One out of four – some say one out of three – women who show up in emergency rooms for treatment are there because of injuries they received from a husband or boyfriend.

And this doesn't just happen to a certain group of people. It happens to women everywhere – all ages, all incomes, all occupations, all races and cultures. It's nothing for you to be ashamed of. It's something for you to do get away from as soon as you can.

But you will have to be careful, and you will need help. Men who are violent when you are living with them often become more violent if they know you are trying to get away. Confide in someone you trust, and find a safe place to go.

There are shelters all over Eastern Kentucky where you can find a safe place to stay. And they can help you in other ways, too – with legal questions, safety planning, child care, counseling, even finding a job.

If you are in danger, call 911. Call the National Domestic Violence Hotline at (800) 799-SAFE. Call your local shelter.

In Rockcastle, Jackson, Laurel, Clay, Knox, Whitley, Bell and Harlan counties, call (800) 755-5348 (crisis line); (606) 256-9511 or (606) 256-2724 (business lines).

In Wolfe, Lee, Owsley, Breathitt, Knott, Letcher, Perry and Leslie counties, call (800) 928-3131(crisis line) or (606) 439-1552 (business line).

In Magoffin, Johnson, Floyd, Martin and Pike counties, call (800) 649-6605 (crisis line) or (606) 285-9079 (business line).

Memorize these numbers. Put them in a safe place. Or call right now.

Good luck. Take care of yourself. You are not alone.

10/20/05

Something for the Pain

I didn't know them well. They joined our church, and for a time they attended almost every Sunday. I liked them. I especially liked her.

She was warm and friendly, easy and pleasant to talk to, with a pretty face and a beautiful smile. He was good-looking, too, but quieter and more distant, a little harder to read.

I heard they had money. He owned a successful business. They had property, a nice home. And they had two beautiful kids who were almost grown, a boy and a girl.

I knew I shouldn't have, but I couldn't help envying them a little. They seemed to have so much.

I don't know when things started to go so wrong for them. I don't know the whole story. Nobody does. And some of the things I heard might not be right. But I know how the story ends. And I know a tragedy when I see one.

They said he'd been hurt on the job, a broken neck or a serious back injury. It gradually got better, but the pain never went away.

Fortunately, or so it seemed at the time, there was an effective new pain medication on the market. The FDA approved it. The pharmaceutical company promoted it. Insurance companies and medical cards paid for it. Doctors prescribed it. And a lot of people started taking it.

It seemed like a good medication. We didn't know

then how easy it was going to be to get it, how easy it was going to be to abuse it, and how easy it was going to be to get hooked. The name of the drug was Oxycontin. Now it's called "hillbilly heroin."

At some point the couple stopped coming to church. I remember hearing that he had become addicted to painkillers. There were rumors of behaviors that sounded out of control, the kind of irrational and desperate acts that characterize addiction. Finally, somebody got him into a treatment facility in Louisville.

She went to see him. On the way back home, in a wreck on I-75 just outside of Lexington, she and one of her sisters were killed. Another sister was seriously injured.

That was a year ago. I never saw him again after that, and the rumors I heard were points on a downward spiral. At church last Sunday, I learned that he had taken his own life.

"He always hated drugs," an old friend of his told me. "Hated what they did to people and what people did to get them. That's why he killed himself. He'd become the thing he hated."

Like I say, I don't know the whole story. I didn't even know them that well. I watched from a safe distance while their lives fell apart. I put five dollars in the love offering. I sang at the funeral. I said the words people say. So sorry . . . anything I can do. But it was all much too little and much too late.

I don't know what we could have done to prevent this tragedy. I do know some things we need to do to prevent others.

We all know that there are drugs and people on drugs all around us. We need to be talking about this in more useful ways than we are. In our families, schools and churches, we need to educate ourselves and our children about drugs and drug addiction. We need good treatment programs here at home. We need stronger law enforcement, better medical care. We need more alternatives for how to earn a living and how to spend one's days. We need to be more compassionate.

We need so many things, it's hard to know where to begin. But we are going to have to try. Or we're going to be hearing a lot more stories like this one.

5/23/02

Occasionally Yours

MUDDLING THROUGH THE YEAR

Big Fat Lies

Come here, you fat little thing you. Yes, you there with the Christmas cookie in one hand and the ham sandwich in the other. Yes, honey, I'm talking to you. Lay that stuff down and waddle over here a minute. There's something I need to say.

Who I'm talking to, of course, is myself. And anybody else this message might apply to. In other words, if the shoe fits but the britches don't, this is for you.

And let's not have any excuses – no whining, no rationalizations, no anything involving cream cheese. Let's forget about caramelizing for a while. Let's decoupage the frying pan and hang it in a decorative manner on the dining room wall. Let's not listen to anything that starts off, "First, you melt a stick of butter."

Let's face it. The hog's been out of the pen a long time now. It has rooted and wallered and foraged all over the countryside, and has eat like – well, like a hog.

It says in the Bible, "She that eateth like a hog shall be like unto a hog. She putteth on fine raiment and goeth forth, and the people shall whisper and say, one to another, She is like unto an hog in fine raiment."

Okay, maybe that's not in the Bible. But that doesn't mean it's not the truth.

I've resolved to lose weight for about forty-seven New Years now, and I think I'm starting to figure something out. It's not just what's in my belly that's making me fat. It's what's in my head. It's all the negative thoughts I keep thinking, all the big fat lies I keep telling myself. Like these:

Big fat lie #1. If something is there and can be eaten, it must be eaten. It must be eaten now, by me, and in its entirety.

Big fat lie #2. If I don't eat every two or three hours, I might die or pass out or get the swim-head or something.

Big fat lie #3. Thinking about exercise, wearing exercise clothing, and purchasing exercise equipment are exercise.

Big fat lie #4. Sugar, mayonnaise and cake are basic foods. Celery, broccoli and fresh fruit are for buying, storing in the produce bin of the refrigerator, then pitching in the garbage when they turn all brown and slimy.

And the biggest fattest lie of all: "I can't lose weight." It might not be easy, it might not be quick, and it might not be fun, but I can do it, and so can you.

So if, like me, you've resolved to lose weight this new year, Lord love you, honey, and good luck.

Remember, it's big fat lies that make us fat. But remember, too, "You shall know the truth, and the truth will make you free."

That's in the Bible.

12/30/02

Death & Taxes

A*nd behold* there went forth a decree from Intermus Revenoous that all the world should be taxed.

And every one went forth to his or her own accountant, or to the accountants of their fathers and mothers before them, bearing with them envelopes, file folders and cardboard boxes which runneth over with receipts, mileage records, cancelled checks and a multitude of other scraps of paper with numbers on them, which during the year that preceedeth had been strewn as if by a mighty wind upon the desk and the floor and in other divers places.

Whilst others taketh not their papers unto an accountant, but spreadeth them forth upon the dining room table, which causeth an unsightly mess upon the table and which causeth none in the household to be able to feast, yea, nor even to snack thereupon until such time as the taxes shall be completed and the mess shall be cleared away.

Those who beareth their papers unto an accountant can then go forth into the daylight as free as the fowls of the air, and go even unto the golf course and playeth golf and unto the shopping centers and purchaseth all manner of earthly goods and, yea, even unto the restaurants and eateth meat which they prepareth not and drinketh from cups which they washeth not.

Whilst their brothers and sisters who taketh not their papers unto an accountant playeth not golf nor buyeth in the marketplace, neither eateth they in restaurants, but sitteth in their houses reading the IRS instruction manual and trying to find exemptions. They sitteth at the table but they eateth not. They readeth but they understandeth not. They seeketh but they findeth not. For whatsoever they doest, it profiteth them nothing, for they must render. And some will be tempted in that day to declare that which is a lie to be the truth, while others will be tempted to curse and swear and some will take strong drink.

But lo I say unto you a day is coming when even those who taketh their papers unto an accountant will likewise be tempted. For when they returneth unto the accountant many will find that the day of reckoning is at hand and they must pay, lo not only unto the federal and unto the state, but unto the accountant also. And then there will be wailing and gnashing of teeth, and many will say in that day, that he that heedeth the words of a politician who runneth for office and sayest unto the people, thou shalt not be taxed, is like unto a man that heareth the sound of the wind and followeth it, even unto the edge of the cliff.

For all must pay, save those with great wealth, who own mighty corporations, who holdeth stock in them and sitteth upon their boards. For they consorteth with the makers of the law. They whisper into the ears of congressmen and senators saying, do this, and lo, it is done, and likewise into the ears of presidents and vice-presidents, saying, make it so, and behold it is so. Thus is the prophesy fulfilled, to him that hath more shall be given, and from him that hath not shall be taken away even that which he hath.

He that possesses much wealth shall pay not much in taxes. But she that teacheth school, she shall pay. And he that laboreth on the highway, he shall pay. And they that worketh in the hospital and the nursing home and the store and the office, they shall pay also, even unto the last farthing.

But their taxes shall not be spent for schools

nor nursing homes. Nor yet for bridges nor highways nor health care nor day care shall they be spent, nor for medicines for the sick nor homes for the homeless. But their taxes shall be spent for bombs which kill and destroy. Which bringeth not security but more fear. Which bringeth not understanding, but more hatred. Which bringeth not joy, but sorrow. Which bringeth not peace, but more war.

4/15/03

The Cornett Family Reunion

We converge one weekend every summer on a park or campground or somebody's back yard, following the signs that say, "Cornett Family Reunion."

We pull up in vans, campers, cars and pickups, with tags from Ohio, Indiana, Kentucky and Tennessee. We come bearing picnic baskets, coolers and Tupperware, and spread their contents out on folding tables.

We come to take our roles in the annual drama, one in which we all keep playing older parts. I remember being a kid at these reunions, running and yelling one minute, turning timid and hiding behind Mother's dress-tail the next. The teenagers still make a show of boredom and disgust, hitting the pop and dessert tables hard, then fleeing at the first threat of hymn singing.

Most of the young adults are too busy, too sophisticated or too far away to come. It's the middle-aged, those of us turning gray of head and vague of waistline, who show up in the greatest numbers.

We come to hear the old stories. How seven Cornett brothers came from England. How William Cornett came into Kentucky on a hunting expedition and found the land so rich and the woods so full of game, he came back to stay, settling near what is now the Letcher - Perry County line.

How two much later Cornett brothers sneaked off to the graveyard one night with sheets over their heads and crouched behind tombstones, waiting to jump out and scare their sister as she walked up the road. How two of their other brothers, overhearing this plot, put sheets over their own heads and crouched behind tombstones, too. And how, when the time was right, they jumped out and scared the first two brothers half out of their silly hides.

We've been laughing about that for a hundred years, though the boys in the story have long since sunk beneath tombstones of their own.

We come to marvel at the mysteries of genetics, that white patch of hair at the temple that sprouts every generation or so, the line of Mamaw's forehead when Doris turns her head. We discover, among far-flung distant relatives, surprising similarities. As a group we present strong, sometimes annoying evidence of a gene for songwriting. A disproportionate number of us write long impassioned letters to the editor. We tend toward nervousness, skinny legs and spirituality.

We come to touch one another. The men shake hands. The women hug. We pass the babies round. Here, let me hold it a while.

We come to remember who we are. Larkin and Jerusia begat Elijah. Elijah and Polly begat Pearl. Pearl and David begat Luther. And right here is where you come in. On a neat genealogical chart, it all makes perfect sense.

We come to sing the old songs. Somebody starts "I'll Fly Away" and by the end of the first verse, we've got three or four parts going, our voices blending in harmonies we did not practice and did not need to. We peer at hymnbooks through the bottoms of bifocals, but this is a pretense. We know these songs by heart.

Some glad morning when this life is o'er, dear friends there'll be no sad farewells. We shall meet where no storm clouds gather. We shall meet on that beautiful shore. If we never meet again this side of heaven, till we meet at Jesus' feet – or next year in Connersville – *God be with you till we meet again.*

7/11/02

Myrtle Beach

M*y sister and I* went to the beach.

We did not take our husbands. Husbands are always saying things like, "It costs too much. I can't take off work. I sunburn badly. I'm allergic to shellfish." We kissed them good-bye and drove away.

At Corbin and Barbourville we were still so close to home, we feared someone might catch us and make us go back and clean house. But somewhere between Pineville and Middlesboro, where the mountains begin to rise more dramatically than at home, we felt we'd escaped. We were on vacation.

Our parents took us on this trip when we were kids. So while it was 2005 and we were two middle-aged women in an SUV with cell phones and directions printed off the Internet, we were also two girls, slightly carsick, in the back seat of a '57 Ford station wagon, on the long curving road from McKee to Myrtle Beach.

The roads are straighter and wider now, but passing through the mountains of Tennessee and North Carolina, you can still see rock-strewn streams and beautiful landscapes – what, in the 1950s, we called "scenery." It is like home but different, familiar but exotic, too. Dad always said, passing through Bean Station, that if we ever had to leave Eastern Kentucky, we'd move to East Tennessee.

When we saw the first palmetto, when the sky opened up and the land flattened and turned red, we knew we were in the South. We had crossed the Appalachian mountain range and were headed downhill to the sea.

Somewhere in the middle of South Carolina, we took a wrong turn, and for a long hour we wandered lost through a string of small sad Southern towns, past deserted fields and factories, past an empty warehouse where weeds grew in the parking lot, past abandoned farmhouses, their blank windows and empty doorframes like the vacant stares of the dead.

There were trailers parked abruptly at the ends of sandy driveways and fast food places and Wal-Marts. It was a lot like home, but flatter.

My cousin Mike, who taught at Jackson County High School, went with a group of students to Myrtle Beach on their senior trip. One boy, seeing the ocean for the first time, seemed disappointed. "It's not as big as I thought it would be," he said.

But to me, on every trip, that first sight of the ocean is all I thought it would be and more. I have a hillbilly heart for Eastern Kentucky, where I was born and have lived most of my life. But somehow I miss the ocean, too, and go running into it that first day, shorts and all, as if I were finally home.

While the ocean was big enough, the rooms we'd rented seemed smaller than they had appeared on the hotel website. But the tiny porch looked right out on the ocean. And so we settled in.

It is important, even when on vacation, to maintain some type of schedule, discipline, and routine. We rose each morning promptly at ten, and proceeded without delay to the porch to drink coffee and observe the ocean. There were decisions to be made: Should we go first to the pool or the beach? Should we walk along the shore, or lie in the sun? Should we have the crab cakes again, or order the entire seafood platter? We discussed these issues earnestly and in detail. We looked at the matter from all angles. We listed the pro's and con's. Then we made our decision, and did not look back.

One afternoon, I sat on the beach in a low lawn chair, under a glorious sunlit sky, watching the waves and listening, letting the wind off the Atlantic Ocean blow my head clean of worries, regrets, aggravations, hurt feelings and petty revenge schemes. I built a sand castle and watched the tide wash it away. The beach is rich in metaphor.

I am older and somewhat taller than I was when I went with my parents to Myrtle Beach. Myrtle Beach is taller, too. Imposing high-rise condos have replaced the modest motels and cottages where we used to stay. Myrtle Beach now is big and crowded, highly commercialized, and more than a little tacky. I like it.

The week went faster than we thought it would. At the end of it, sunburned, relaxed, and not quite ready to go home, my sister and I vowed to come back next year. Maybe we'd bring our husbands.

Maybe not.

7/10/05

From Every Mountainside

Over the long hot Fourth of July weekend, my husband and I worked around the place. We ate a lot of ice cream and potato salad. We sweated a lot.

Motorcycles roared by. Firecrackers exploded in the distance. And Friday night we went to Lee County to the fireworks show.

Just at dusk, at Happy Top, Kentucky, on an old strip mine site outside of Beattyville, hundreds of vehicles lined up, facing west. Couples, children, teenagers and grandparents leaned against their cars, or sat talking quietly in lawn chairs in the backs of pickup trucks.

Suddenly booms of sound shook the evening air and drove all other thoughts right out of our heads. When the first fireworks exploded into colors and fell like shooting stars against the night sky, we all let out one long musical "Aaaaaaaah."

A whistle, a pop, and a small explosion overhead blossomed into a giant ball of red and green. A little girl's voice yelled in delight, "It's a flower!"

I remembered that the Japanese word for fireworks means "fire flowers." And I remembered another fireworks show I'd seen another summer, half a world away. In Japan during the festival of Obon, families visit the graves of their dead. They go to the temple to pray, and then they celebrate, with music, dancing, and fireworks.

It was a little like our Memorial Day, a little like

the Fourth of July. I learned on that trip how much alike people are, no matter where they live. And I learned how much people in Japan love their country.

On the Fourth of July, we feel patriotic. We feel proud of all that is good about America.

But that doesn't mean we have to look down on other countries. It doesn't mean we can't criticize our government or question its leaders. It doesn't mean we close our eyes to all we still need to do.

Patriotism is a high allegiance, but there are even higher ones – allegiance to God, to all His creatures and all His creation, allegiance to what is right.

At the fireworks show at Happy Top, the deejay played patriotic music: "The Star Spangled Banner," Lee Greenwood singing "I'm Proud to be an American," Sousa's famous march. Then, just before the final "God Bless America," he played what may have been the most patriotic song of all, Garth Brooks' "We Shall Be Free":

When the last child cries for a crust of bread –
When there's shelter over the poorest head –
When the last thing we notice is the color of skin –
When the skies and the oceans are clean again –
When we're free to love anyone we choose –
When this world's big enough for all different views –
When we all can worship from our own kind of pews –
Then, we shall be free.

7/7/03

Wildflowers, Women & Song

E*arly fall,* and the fields below the barn are thick with wildflowers. In a jungle of green fading to brown, cardinal flowers blossom, blood-red. Goldenrod, heavy with yellow, bends over mistflowers, blue lobelia, white and purple asters. Giant bloomed heads of joe-pye, queen of the meadow, rise on tall straight stalks. Jewel weed adorns the creek banks. And everywhere there is ironweed.

With its tiny blossoms of deep purple, ironweed looks delicate, but its stalk is surprisingly tough. Try picking a bouquet of ironweed, and you'll find yourself reaching for your pocket knife, or running back to the house for a pair of scissors. Ironweed is a good name for it.

Ironweed is a good name, too, for an Appalachian women's arts festival held every September, when ironweed is in bloom. Last week at a 4-H Camp outside Abingdon, Virginia, women from all over the Appalachian region came together to share their art.

We sang songs we all knew and songs we had written ourselves. We played guitars, autoharps, banjos and drums. We displayed paintings, photographs and handmade jewelry. We danced. We read poems, told stories and performed plays about our mothers, our grandmothers, about other Appalachian women who inspired us, and about our own lives.

The Ironweed Festival is sponsored by the

Appalachian Women's Alliance, a diverse network of women in seven Appalachian states, working on issues that affect the lives of Appalachian women, including racism, domestic violence, and economic justice. The website (www.appalachianwomen.org) says, "We are black, white and Cherokee, rural and urban, straight and gay, seven to seventy."

The beautiful hills of southwest Virginia provided the perfect backdrop for the festival, and, between arts events, Abingdon proved a great place to explore. Unlike a lot of towns, Abingdon has preserved its historic buildings and turned them into restaurants, bookstores, art galleries, craft shops and antique stores.

And Abingdon is home to the Barter Theater, where you can see professional plays year round. I saw "Grace Moore, the Tennessee Nightingale." Grace Moore, it turns out, was a girl from Jellico, Tennessee, who grew up to become an internationally known star of opera, popular music, Hollywood and Broadway. I recognized her face and her voice from old movies. I'd never known she was from just over the ridge.

There are other Appalachian women who, like Grace Moore, left the mountains and worked successfully in the arts. But we hardly ever hear about them. Many more never got the chance to develop their talents, and they withered and died on the vine.

But most Appalachian women artists expressed themselves in the few venues that were open to them – quilting, gardening, sewing, church music, storytelling. Like fall wildflowers, they bloomed in rocky ground – hearty as goldenrod, showy as cardinal flowers, sturdy as ironweed.

9/29/03

Thousands of Husbands Disappear

E*very year about this time,* my husband disappears. He goes into the TV room with a can of peanuts and a bag of potato chips, and I don't see him again till the end of football season.

I've learned not to go in there when he's like this. There's no sign that says KEEP OUT or NO WOMEN ALLOWED. I've just found from long experience that there's not much point in trying to communicate with him right now.

I used to try to talk to my husband while he was watching football. He would make some token effort to acknowledge my presence in the room. He'd even pretend to be listening to what I was saying. But his heart wasn't in it. His eyes flickered nervously back and forth with the action on the screen. His responses were even more inappropriate than usual.

I could be in the middle of a long complex monolog about my innermost thoughts and feelings, the accent color in the bathroom, or something very interesting my great-grandmother once said, and my normally reticent and dignified husband would suddenly leap to his feet and emit a loud primitive howl, culminating with, "DID YOU SEE THAT???!!!???!!"

I didn't see it. The next minute he'd amble off in search of more potato chips, leaving me alone with a blaring commercial.

I'm surprised at how emotional men can be about

football, when nothing in real life seems to excite them that much. Present them with a seven-course dinner and you're lucky if you get a peck on the cheek and a mumbled, "That's good, honey." Fire, flood, famine, debt, disease, death and disaster – men meet these with a combination of peevishness and philosophical detachment.

But turn on a football game, and they suddenly become creatures of emotion. They soar to the heights of ecstasy. They plunge to the depths of despair. They hover at the brink of hope. They are awash with righteous indignation. They are stunned with disbelief. Their faces are animated. They dance in celebration. They writhe in anguish. In short, they bear little resemblance to the steady, reserved and sometimes boring men we have come to know and love.

I don't get what the big deal is about football. To me it looks like a bunch of guys with plastic shoulders and war paint on their faces running, throwing the ball, and then all jumping on top of one another in a big disgusting heap. The ones at the bottom of the heap get hurt and have to limp to the sidelines or be carried off on stretchers.

As soon as the wounded are off the field, the rest of them start back doing just like they had been before, running and throwing and heaping up again, as if they hadn't learned a thing from seeing what just happened to those other guys.

They do this for hours on end, trying to get the football and keep it away from each other. Why don't they just take turns playing with it? Or why doesn't somebody just get another ball?

I told you I didn't get it. One Sunday afternoon a long time ago, in a brief misguided effort to be somebody else and to share in my husband's interests, I sat on the couch in front of a football game and let him try to explain it to me. I still didn't' get it. It was complicated without being interesting.

Ever since then during football season, we go our

separate ways for a while. I try not to come up with a lot of ideas for fall home improvement projects. I try not to initiate discussions about sensitive matters he doesn't want to talk about. I try not to give lectures on the inherent violence and superficiality of organized football.

Some people say football is a way men have of acting out their tendencies toward competitiveness, control, aggression and war. So in a way I'm in favor of football. At least it's better than the real thing.

So there might be some violence on our TV during football season. But other than that, everything's peaceful at our house. He's watching football. I'm reading or playing the piano or talking to my sister on the phone.

Later on my husband and I will start doing things together again, things we can both understand and appreciate. Like UK basketball.

8/29/02

How to Tell It's Fall

One year at this time, I was visiting an elementary school in Barbourville, teaching writing to fourth graders. I wanted them to notice and write about all the changes taking place around us with the changing of the seasons.

So I said something like, "How do you know when it's fall? I mean, if you didn't have a calendar, and if nobody said anything about it, how would you know it was fall?"

They looked at me like they were beginning to suspect I might be really really odd. But with just a little more prodding, they picked up their pencils and began to write. Here's some of what they said.

How to Tell It's Fall

In fall my dad makes chili.
My mom gets the covers out.
My Uncle Frankie goes hunting.
My father and my brother and I make a fodder shock.
We get pumpkins out of the garden.
My mom cooks soup beans.
We gather firewood.
Dad wears a coat.
We turn on the heaters.
We watch football.
The days get shorter.

I look up and see birds flying south.
There's frost on the grass when you first get up.
Leaves fall off the trees and blow on people's porches.
I pile up leaves and jump in them.
Mom's flowers die.
You have to go to the attic and get your sweaters out.
You hear guns in the woods.
You see all kinds of colors of trees.
It's cold and it rains.
I get sick.
The windows sweat.
The creek has leaves in it.
Dad gets fatter.
We watch scary movies. I get scared and go
        jump in the bed with Papaw.
It's dark when Dad gets home.
Everybody talks about basketball.
Mom says, You have to take a jacket.
We pick greens.
Everybody's got on sweat pants.
Dad puts black plastic over the grill.
You can see sharp limbs on trees.
We don't have to mow.
We take the tobacco down and strip it.
I've got a big bag of Halloween candy under my bed.
Big Pilgrims are taped on the walls at school.
Me and my brother start thinking about Christmas.

10/7/02

∽

Thanks a Lot

At this time of year we remember, however
inaccurately, the Pilgrims who came to this continent
from England in search of the freedom to worship in
their own way, to wear big buckles on their hats and
shoes, and to escape religious persecution, in order that
they might turn around and persecute somebody else.

We remember the Indians, who taught the Pilgrims how to plant corn, which for some reason the
Pilgrims could not figure out for themselves.

We remember Pocahontas and a couple of guys
named John, and Pocahontas saying something like,
Why don't you speak for yourself, John? Well, maybe
we don't really remember that.

We remember Thanksgivings past, when the
women would go into the kitchen and cook for days on
end to come up with a meal that could truly be called
a feast. We remember this today as we open the box of
Stove Top stuffing, slither the cranberry sauce out of the
can, slide the frozen pumpkin pies into the oven, and
dollop out the Kool Whip.

And in spite of everything, we remember that we
really do have a lot to be thankful for.

Most of the time, we tend to focus on what's
wrong with our lives – that one person at work who
drives us nuts, disturbing events in the news, money
worries, health problems, aggravations, disappointments and losses. It's easy to list all the things that are

wrong.

Thanksgiving reminds us of how much is right, starting with the fact that we are still here, after all, for another Thanksgiving.

Me, I'm thankful for coffee, cornbread and music. I'm thankful for the hugs I get from kids when I go to their school to tell stories. I'm thankful for a warm, dry, safe place to sleep at night. A lot of people in the world don't have that.

I'm thankful for trees, friends, bathtubs, libraries, the radio, and lemons. I'm thankful for my dogs, who run and leap and dance with joy when they see me coming. I am truly thankful for Dwight Yoakum.

I'm thankful for colors, hymnbooks, creeks, old barns, rain and rocks. I'm thankful for house shoes, art museums, elastic waistbands, my preacher and my neighbors. I'm thankful somebody figured out how to make lightweight glasses for the really really really nearsighted.

I'm thankful for poetry, candles, my family, morning light and afternoon naps. I'm thankful that my great-grandparents bought this place, and that my grandparents and then my uncle held on to it, even when it was hard.

I'm thankful for any and all examples of humor, healing, forgiveness, tolerance, kindness and courage.

I'm thankful for all the people who've written, called, and stopped me in the grocery store to tell me they like my columns.

And I'm thankful to you for reading these words. Happy Thanksgiving.

11/28/02

Corrections & Clarifications

ꝏ

*N*ote: This column you are about to read, I
made it all up. Any resemblance to actual persons and
events is purely coincidental and does not constitute
grounds for legal action. Thank you.

ꝏ

From time to time it is necessary for THE LOCAL
NEWS to run a list of corrections and clarifications.

An error appeared in the captions of two photographs published on page 7 of the November 18 issue
of THE LOCAL NEWS. The captions were reversed. The
photo of sheriff's deputies holding several large mari-
juana plants seized in a raid on a local underground
growing operation should not have read, "Ladies Garden
Club Displays Fruits of Labor."

Likewise, the photo of local garden club members
shown smiling beside poinsettias they had grown to
place in public buildings for the holiday season ought
not to have read, "Growers Busted in Midnight Raid.
Cash and Weapons Seized."

Green Flem of Flem's Branch would like to state
that he is not the same Green Flem that was appre-
hended October 31 following a high speed chase by local
and state law enforcement authorities and lodged in
the county detention center on charges of DUI, wanton
endangerment, terroristic threatening, resisting arrest,
lewd and lascivious behavior, parole violation and theft

by unlawful taking. We would like to apologize to the Reverend Flem, his family and congregation for any inconvenience. Rev. Flem asks us to further state that there is no truth to the rumor that the church has split as a result of this misunderstanding, and the potluck supper scheduled for December 12 in the Fellowship Hall will go on as planned.

Eva Young would like to clarify for the record that there was an error in her age as it appeared in a caption accompanying her picture in the Society section of THE LOCAL NEWS November 25. Miss Young is 43 years old and not 143 as stated. The staff of THE LOCAL NEWS would like to apologize to Miss Young once again and ask her to please stop calling the newspaper office in regard to this matter.

The November 11 issue of THE LOCAL NEWS contained an exclusive interview with longtime former local politician Ernest Knott, recently indicted by the grand jury in connection with the shooting of a political opponent. Knott's attorney wishes to state that when his client said, "I just wisht I'd a had a better bead on him," his client was speaking off the record, under duress, without benefit of an attorney present and furthermore was not in his right mind at the time.

Knott's attorney requests that the public, particularly those persons currently eligible for jury pool, should forget they ever read that.

12/1/03

What'll We Do for the Christmas Play?

If Halloween is just around the corner, then Thanksgiving must be somewhere on the next street, and Christmas just two blocks down. That means, among other things, that it's time to start working on the church Christmas play.

This is an area in which I have some experience. When I moved my membership, I hadn't been a member of the church five minutes before somebody said, "You can direct the church Christmas play!" I was honored. I was flattered. I was incredibly naïve.

At the first practice, I asked one little fellow if he would be a shepherd. "Sure," he replied, "a German shepherd." And he barked, Ruff ruff.

When you are the director of the church Christmas play, you hear yourself saying odd things like, "Balthazar, the baby Jesus is not a football. Put him back in the manger right now and go get your myrrh. Mary, honey, spit out your gum. Shepherds, quiet please, I can't hear the angels singing."

But you know, we had a wonderful Christmas play that year. Because it doesn't really matter if the wise men trip over their bathrobes on the way to the manger scene. It doesn't matter if some of the angels get sleepy and run off the stage to nestle, wings and all, in their grandmothers' laps. It doesn't even matter if Joseph is inaudible, the Virgin Mary blows bubbles, and the shepherds bark, Ruff ruff.

The wonder, the magic and the mystery of the story of the first Christmas still shine through. Because they are in the story itself.

That's why I don't really get it when people ask, What play are we doing for Christmas this year? I don't think there's much we can do to improve on the original story, or on the way it's told in the Book of Luke.

We don't need toys that come to life. We don't need to examine the birth of Christ from the point of view of a mouse. We don't need to take "a humorous look at life in Israel in the first century A.D." We don't need to frighten people with the idea that they might get killed in a car wreck and go straight to hell on Christmas Eve. We don't need to put on straw hats and bibbed overalls and stomp around like refugees from "Hee Haw," demeaning our Appalachian ancestors, our neighbors and ourselves.

The son of God comes to earth, born in a stable to a poor, unmarried young woman. Angels appear to shepherds. Wise men follow a mysterious star. King Herod orders his soldiers to kill all Jewish boy babies. Mary and Joseph flee with the baby. And He grows up to be the Savior of the world.

Now that's a story, people. Let's do that one. Ruff ruff.

10/6/03

Spirits of Christmas Past

The house we lived in the Christmas I was ten had a big picture window. My parents bought a shiny aluminum tree and put it on a table in front of the picture window and decorated it all in blue and shone a spotlight on it with a wheel that turned and made the tree appear to change colors. We thought this very beautiful, and very modern.

My Dad had grown up in Jackson County, my Mother in Clay, and their Christmases as children had been modest ones. Dad had eight brothers and sisters. He remembered being happy to get candy and an orange for Christmas, and maybe a pair of socks.

Mother remembered being a little frightened on Christmas. In those days, some of the men marked the occasion by getting drunk and riding up and down the road on horses, shouting and firing weapons in the air.

One year when she and her brother Millard were little, he found their Christmas presents hidden on top of the pump organ. He told her this proved once and for all there was no Santa Claus. She hauled off and slapped him right sharp across the jaw.

When my sister Lynne and I were kids, our parents wanted us to have a good Christmas. They didn't overdo it, but they always gave each of us one really nice thing – a record player, a miniature stove, a Cinderella watch, a toy piano or a jewelry box with a tiny ballerina inside.

After opening our presents at home on Christmas morning, we'd head for Mamaw Gabbard's house at Gray Hawk. Since Dad's family was so big, everybody didn't buy everybody else a present. We drew names, like we did at school. But we got together on Christmas day, a big rowdy crowd of us, and there was quite a bit of laughing that went on, and singing and candy-making and Rook-playing, and roving gangs of cousins running back and forth through the house.

It'd be dark by the time we got to Teges. Pa would have cut a big cedar from the hillside, and the cold clean scent of it, with winter rain and wind still in it, met us at the door.

These grandparents kept a store, and every year my sister and I could each count on getting a big beautiful doll for Christmas, which my grandmother would have got "off the drummer," she said.

After opening our presents, we'd settle down for Christmas supper – country ham, chicken and dumplings, shucky beans, apple stack cake, hand pies.

Finally, we pulled our chairs up to the coal grate for cracked walnuts and quiet talk, and in that warmth and flickering light, grew drowsy and content. For the moment, we were safe and full and at peace with one another.

For the moment, we were together.

12/26/02

Christmas Journey

***I**t was the first time* I'd flown since September 11. I'm not afraid to fly, I kept telling myself.

Every day hundreds of planes carrying thousands of passengers take off from airports all over the country and safely reach their destinations, I kept telling myself.

You're a lot more likely to be killed in a car than an airplane, I kept telling myself. Especially if you drive on the Daniel Boone Parkway.

My son had asked me to come to Austin for a visit. And a mother bear, as you know, will climb steep mountains, ford swift streams and fly through the air in the middle of a terrorist alert to get to her cub, even if her cub is a 6'4" thirty-year-old radio announcer.

I made my reservations. I wasn't going to be one of those people afraid to fly this Christmas, I kept telling myself.

But by the time my husband and I got to the Cincinnati airport, I wasn't feeling so brave. Something was wrong here, and it showed.

The last time I'd been in this airport, an ordinary Sunday afternoon before September 11, there'd hardly been room to stand. Now, two Saturdays before Christmas, when the airport should have been bustling with college students, grandmothers, and everybody else trying to get somewhere for the holidays, the place seemed almost deserted. Men in uniform lined the hallways and surrounded the check-in counters, rifles at the ready.

Somehow I did not find this comforting.

When I've flown before, my husband always walks me to the gate, holds my hand while we wait, kisses me good-bye as I get on the plane. But now only those people who are actually flying are allowed past the security checkpoints. They want you to show up two hours before take-off. So after everything in your purse, bags and pockets has been looked at suspiciously by bored and surly airport personnel, you've still got plenty of time to get nervous.

I find my gate and sit, trying unsuccessfully to relax till my flight is called. When they tell us to line up for the flight to Austin, there's a second when I almost bolt. I could just not get on the plane, I think. Then I remember I've got nowhere else to go.

My husband is already headed back down the interstate toward Oneida. If I get on the plane I'll be in Austin in three hours. If I chicken out, I'm stuck in the Cincinnati airport for at least six. This is bound to arouse suspicion, and could possibly get me interrogated, and even searched in places I prefer to remain private. I take a deep breath and get on the plane.

Inside, away from the spooky airport and the armed guards, the atmosphere seems normal, almost cozy. Just a bunch of ordinary folks going somewhere they want to go for Christmas, going to see somebody they love. I adjust my reading light, my seat belt, my attitude. I settle in and settle down. I'm going to see somebody I love, too.

Most flights I've been on the past few years have been packed tight as sardine cans. But today there are plenty of empty seats. We spread out. We can each have our own row. Some people claim the aisle seats. They like to stretch their legs and read the paper. I move to a window.

The plane takes off and I'm looking down at a crazy quilt of brown and green patches. The Ohio River, muddy with the recent rains, snakes its way through flat fields and honeycomb subdivisions.

Then we're climbing through clouds and I can't see the quilt or the snake anymore. Suddenly we break through the clouds to a vast silent world where there is only sunshine, bright blue sky, and, as far as you can see, a kingdom of mountains, plains and castles made all of pure white clouds glistening in the sun.

Then I remember what I've always loved about flying. You've escaped a while from your everyday life. You've overcome gravity. You've entered a world that is incredibly beautiful and a little bit magic.

It's an evening flight, headed southwest. Night follows us close all the way, trying to catch up, but we keep just ahead of it, flying into a perpetual sunset.

There's a light rain in Austin as we come in just at dusk, and something about the rain and the twilight together wraps the lights of the airport in a golden glow that stops my breath for a second.

Inside the terminal, I look past the crowds of strangers and the men with rifles to see my son waiting for me, smiling, happy to see me, his long arms stretched wide for a welcoming hug.

If I hadn't flown this Christmas, I'd have missed that. I'd have missed finding out how friendly the people in Austin are. I'd have missed the great food and great music they have there. I'd have missed the good feeling you get when you do something you're a little bit scared to do.

The Christmas story has more than one lesson. If the shepherds and wise men had played it safe and stayed home, they'd have missed seeing the baby Jesus.

"And the angel said unto them, Fear not."

1/10/02

202

A Triplet Christmas

I've still not got my house straightened out from Christmas.

Our triplet grandsons, aged 21 months, came to visit. When they left a few days later, there was hardly anything in the house – and that's including the furniture – that was in the same place it had been when they came.

We'd tried to put everything sharp or toxic – or anything we really wanted to keep – up high out of toddler reach. This left the rooms with a peculiar bipolar appearance, the top half cluttered and Victorian-looking, the lower half spare, like Shakertown.

But the boys got into things we hadn't anticipated. They pushed the walls of their play yard over and were free. They pulled the books off the bookshelves. They climbed up in the windowsills and banged on the glass. They used the piano for a ladder. They put their arms down in the dog's water bucket. They crawled under the bed and got stuck.

At supper, Luke threw his peas back over his shoulder one at a time, hollering "No!" to each pea. Leo turned his sippy-cup upside down and watched the apple juice drip out onto his tray, then splashed it with the flat of his hand. Ace smeared yogurt on his face, then wore the plastic yogurt cup for a hat. They all preferred crackers and cookies to meat and vegetables, and they all threw their food and dishes on the floor. Then Leo threw up.

You'd think they would have been tired after all that.

At bedtime we gave them warm baths and bottles, wrapped them in soft blankets, turned down the lights, then rocked them while singing soothing lullabies. This stimulated them to climb up on the tops of our heads and shout out their vocabulary words: Dog! Book! Bottle! Mama! DaDa! No! Quack Quack!

In between resisting sleep and throwing food and courting danger, they played and laughed and sang and danced and were generally amazing and wonderful.

At the end of the visit, as their van pulled away, headed back to Louisville, I stood amidst the chaos of my life and wept, not because my house looked like three small tornadoes had roared through, not even because I was badly in need of a hot bath, a healthy meal, and a good night's sleep. I was crying because they were gone.

All your life you hear the jokes about grandparents, how nutty they are about their grandchildren, always bragging that THEIRS are the cutest and the brightest and the sweetest, always carrying those pictures around, forcing people to look at them.

This always seemed to me just part of the inevitable senility that overtakes people after a certain age – harmless, funny, and maybe a little pathetic.

But now that I've joined the club, I totally get it. All of us grandparents are absolutely correct. Our grandchildren are indeed the sweetest and the cutest and the brightest, because they are the cutest and brightest and sweetest things we have seen in a long dreary time, and are likely to ever see again. No matter what else we don't know or understand or remember anymore, we have lived long enough to know that.

By the time my husband got home that night, I'd cleared paths to the bed, the bathroom and the kitchen. The laundry room was still a mountain range of dirty clothes and linens. The kitchen counters were stacked with dirty dishes, the hall table with unopened mail.

Tiny torn-off bits of Christmas wrapping paper littered the floor, some of them stuck firmly with the adhesive that forms when you mix yogurt, apple juice and peas. The faint smell of vomit lingered in the air.

"Everything's a mess," I told my husband. "And so am I."

"I know," he said. "I'd take them back in a second."

Me, too.

1/12/06

They Don't Make 'em Like That Anymore

MEMORIES & GOODBYES

Elvis, Happy Birthday in Heaven

It was raining when we got to Memphis. This trip was a Christmas present from my son, something I'd been wanting a long time – a pilgrimage to Graceland.

We parked in the lot across from the mansion and walked to the visitors center to get our tickets. Even on this gloomy weekday not long before Christmas, the place was busy. More than half a million people a year come here.

We ordered a burger and fries at the Rockabilly Café while we waited for the next shuttle bus. Elvis sang to us over the P.A. system, "Blue Christmas," "Merry Christmas, Baby" and the sexiest Christmas carol of all time, "Santa Claus is Back in Town."

On your way to the shuttle bus, they snap your picture in front of a fake Graceland. But when you cross Elvis Presley Boulevard and see the real gate, the figure with guitar and the eighth notes wrought in iron, you know you're really there.

Graceland is decorated for Christmas, with a nativity scene on the front lawn, and further back, Christmas trees formed by blue lights. On the foyer staircase, a red poinsettia stands at either end of each white-carpeted step. There's something about the stairs that makes you think Elvis might come down them any minute.

We put on the headsets they give us and start the

tour. We look at Elvis' living room, his parents' bed-room, his dining room, kitchen, music room, TV room, pool room, and "jungle room" den. In one room, there's a big round bed covered with white fur.

I cannot believe it. I am actually standing there looking at the black leather outfit Elvis wore in the '68 Comeback Special. There are other costumes, too, as well as jewelry, photographs, and mementoes from Elvis' thirty-three movies, his concerts, his TV appearances, and from his Army days.

Behind the house are Elvis' racquetball court, business office, and automobile museum. The trophy building shows his gold and platinum records and other awards, and the three Grammy's he won, all for gos-pel. If you've never heard Elvis sing gospel, you'll want to remedy that right away. After his concerts, they say, he'd sing gospel all night long.

Then all of a sudden you're outside again, and it's almost over. You pass the swimming pool and walk to-ward the Meditation Garden, and there it is, Elvis' grave, alongside those of his parents and his grandmother.

Somehow, after the mansion and the trophy building and the giant photographs, Elvis' grave seems surprisingly small. But of course it isn't. It's the normal size, not for a god or a devil, but for a person. The stone reads simply: Elvis Aaron Presley. January 8, 1935 - August 16, 1977.

Happy Birthday, Elvis.

1/8/03

Remembering Rosemary

"She's from Kentucky,"** somebody would always say whenever Rosemary Clooney came on TV back in the 1950s. We didn't really know her, but we felt like we did, and we were proud of her.

When she died earlier this year, I thought about how much Rosemary Clooney had meant to a lot of us in Kentucky, how much we needed her, and how much we'll miss her.

In the '50s, like today, Kentuckians were the butt of countless hillbilly, briar and redneck jokes. Rosemary Clooney showed that Kentuckians aren't really like the people in the jokes, that we're not all cut from the same cloth, that given the chance, we can do about anything.

Blonde and beautiful, with a golden voice and an easy manner, Rosemary Clooney was a star who was easy to like. Even in gowns by Edith Head, she radiated a girl-next-door quality. Somehow she made you feel as if she were someone you knew and were perfectly at ease with.

That quality and the fact that she was from Kentucky made her more than just another movie star, especially to girls growing up in Kentucky in the 1950s. On the big flat rock in front of our grandparents' farmhouse on Teges Creek, my sister and I pretended we lived in a New York penthouse, serving martinis to elegant gentlemen, dancing and singing our way through life in gowns by Edith Head.

After the movie *White Christmas* came out, we mimicked Vera-Ellen's dance steps and memorized the words Clooney sang to "Sisters."

Lord help the mister who comes between me and my sister
And Lord help the sister who comes between me and my man

Rosemary Clooney was everything we thought we wanted to be then. She was beautiful, talented, rich and famous, and she was nice. She showed us possibilities and gave us hope. She was from Kentucky, and if she could make it, maybe we could, too.

❧

I forgot about Rosemary Clooney for a long time after that, and so did a lot of other people. The loud advent of rock-n-roll pushed her style of singing to the periphery of the music industry and of the national consciousness. In her twenties, she'd had a string of popular hits – "Hey There," "Come On-A My House," "This Ole House," "Half as Much," "Beautiful Brown Eyes." She'd hosted two television shows, *The Rosemary Clooney Show* and *The Lux Show Starring Rosemary Clooney.*

But for much of the middle part of her life, she wasn't performing so much as dealing with a series of life crises – financial problems, a difficult marriage and divorce, issues of abandonment left over from childhood, and a deepening dependence on prescription drugs.

She was with her friend Robert Kennedy the night he was killed, which proved to be a kind of last straw. "The whole country had a nervous breakdown in the 1960s," she said once. "I just had mine in public."

But Rosemary Clooney came back. She went through therapy, got off drugs, married an old sweetheart, and re-established herself as a singer, this time on her own terms. She resumed an active touring and performing schedule, and in the late 1970s began a series of recordings of American standards which critics have praised and fans have loved.

Rosemary Clooney came back. That's another reason we've needed her and will miss her. When I saw her perform in Louisville a few years ago, she still had that quality of making the audience feel as if we were all old friends. And she still had that magical voice, impossible to describe, but familiar and necessary somehow, and somehow exactly right.

She was older and fatter than the Rosemary Clooney I saw on TV as a kid. But since I was older and fatter myself, I found this encouraging. She'd gone through hard times. She'd shown human frailty. She'd had problems and disappointments and losses, like the rest of us. And she'd come back. If she could make it, maybe we could, too.

9/12/02

꿍

Remembering Lee Howard

A̲t her funeral service in Manchester, she
was honored for being a loving and generous person and
a good daughter. But Lee Howard, who died suddenly
at the age of 51, was much more than that.

A professional sociologist, she'd worked at the
atomic energy plant in Oak Ridge, Tennessee, and later
as a vocational counselor in Portland, Oregon. She'd
completed a masters degree in theology and was prepar-
ing to become an Episcopal priest. And she was a poet.

The publication in 1980 of her first book of poems, *The Last Unmined Vein*, was an important event in
Appalachian literature. With that book, Howard opened
a door, and other poets followed her through it.

I first heard Lee Howard read her poems at a
Women Writers Conference at the University of Kentucky in 1980. I did not know the tall, dark-haired
woman who stood up to read that day, but the voices
and stories and concerns in her poems were familiar to
me. They were straight out of Clay County, Kentucky.

Lee Howard showed me, not just that a girl from
Southeastern Kentucky can grow up to be a poet, but
how to do it – by tapping into the power of those familiar
mountain voices.

Her fellow poet and longtime friend George Ella
Lyon read a tribute poem to Lee at graveside services at
Piney Grove.

Another Appalachian author, Gurney Norman,

professor of creative writing at UK, had this to say about Howard after learning of her death:

Lee Howard was one of the most dynamic new poets to emerge in the Appalachian region in the late 1970s and early 1980s. In her life and in her work, she was a force. Her great spirit and powerful language made her an indispensable writer in what has been called the Appalachian literary renaissance of the 1970s and 1980s.

For one thing, she knew more about the lives of mountain people who worked with their hands than anyone. Her writing was faithful to the speech of the common people. Many of her poems were storytelling poems, narratives in which the lives of real people in a real place were made vivid.

She wrote with such gusto, there was such force in her words, you could not read her work without being affected. Hearing her read her work aloud was an unforgettable experience.

Lee inspired more people than she knew. She was better known as a poet than most people who knew her realized. Her influence was widespread. She was utterly honest in her writing, and truly generous in her dealings with other writers and people.

Lee Howard had a beautiful soul, a tender heart, and courage. It is crucial that her work be gathered in a well-made book, or books, for she certainly lives on through her words.

5/4/03

Goodbye, Sweetheart

You know the picture. Lyndon Johnson with
his right hand raised, his left on the Bible, standing between Jackie and Lady Bird on Air Force One, November
22, 1963. In the lower left corner of the picture, a dark-
haired man holds a tape recorder up to LBJ as he is
being sworn in as President.

That was Malcolm Kilduff, then Assistant White
House Press Secretary and Acting Press Secretary on
the ill-fated trip to Dallas. It fell to him to make the
official announcement that nobody wanted to hear.

Mac Kilduff would live another forty years after
that. He died last week in Jackson. For the rest of his
life he would be known as the man in the famous picture, the man who announced the death of the president. Hundreds of reporters, oral historians and other
researchers interviewed him over the years, particularly
on each anniversary of the JFK assassination, asking
the same questions, wanting to hear the story again.

Mac accepted his role and he played it with dignity. He knew the story was important, and he'd talk
about it if you asked him. But he wasn't usually the
one to bring it up.

There was more to him than that. He had a whole
life, a full life. And he didn't need to trade on his Kennedy connection to know who he was.

For the last twenty-five years Mac Kilduff lived in
Beattyville, his wife Rosemary's hometown. For a

decade he edited the town's newspaper, *The Beattyville Enterprise.* On the walls of the newspaper office, you can still see the awards the paper won during the time Mac was there, as well as the bullet holes left when a disgruntled reader shot into the office where Mac was working late one night.

As a young man in Washington, D.C., he'd had to drop out of college when his father died, and work two full-time jobs to support the family. One job was at a drug store; the other was at the State Department, pasting photos into passports. He worked his way up from there.

He was a Navy veteran, active in the Episcopal Church, the Kiwanis Club, and a dozen other organizations. He had four children, one of whom had died at four years old.

He was a complex person, kindly, cynical, charming, outspoken, brilliant and funny. We talked on the phone sometimes, and even after his health began to fail, he still managed to be outrageous and even a little flirty.

I liked his voice over the phone, a deep gentle bass, and I liked it that just before he hung up, he always said the same thing: Goodbye, Sweetheart.

Keep it short, he advised me once about column-writing. Okay, Mac.

And Goodbye, Sweetheart.

3/10/03

Aunt Molly Jackson

She **was born** Mary Magdalene Garland in Clay County, Kentucky, in 1880. But anybody who studies the history of folk music, coalmining, or the labor movement in America knows her by a different name – Aunt Molly Jackson.

The oldest child of Oliver Garland and Deborah Robinson Garland, Molly spent the first years of her life on Rader's Creek in Clay County. The family then went to live at a coal camp in Laurel County, where Deborah died when Molly was just six.

Molly later became a nurse and midwife. Women who did that work were usually called "Granny," but Molly was so young when she started, they called her "Aunt" instead, and the name stuck.

Married to a miner, she lived in coal camps in Knox, Bell and Harlan counties. Miners could make a good living for their families in the 1920s, but when the Depression hit, wages went down to just pennies a ton, and that was paid in scrip, good only at the company store. There were few safety regulations in those days, and little or no compensation for the families of men killed or maimed in the mines.

The miners struck for better pay and safer working conditions, and Aunt Molly contributed to the cause with songs she wrote and sang herself, like "Poor Miner's Farewell," "Hard Times in Coleman's Mines" and "Hungry Ragged Blues."

When coal operators broke the strike, its leaders, including Aunt Molly, were forced to leave Kentucky. She went to New York City to live in December 1931, and was befriended by writer Theodore Dreiser, who admired her eloquence in describing the plight of Kentucky miners.

Well known in the 1930s as a folk singer and spokesperson for working Americans, Aunt Molly Jackson is still well known today among scholars of American history and music. There's a book about her, and two different records of her songs. She died in California in 1960.

They tell it that one time, at a Harlan County coal camp in the darkest days of the Depression, with babies dying of starvation and children all around her crying for food, Aunt Molly, without a cent, marched into the company store and ordered a sack of groceries. When the clerk handed them over, she told him she'd be back to pay the bill, but she had some hungry children to feed first. When he tried to stop her, she pulled a .38 out of her pocket and backed out the door.

She'd barely given out the food when a deputy sheriff showed up to arrest her. After hearing her story, he paid the bill himself.

Aunt Molly probably still has relatives around Southeastern Kentucky. As far as I know, she's no kin to me. If she were, I'd be proud to claim her.

12/12/02

They Don't Make 'em
Like My Daddy Anymore

*L*oretta Lynn came to Hazard in 1976, and sang at the old high school gymnasium. I sat by myself way up in the bleachers, singing along to "Coal Miner's Daughter," "Fist City" and "If You're Lookin' at Me, You're Lookin' at Country." But halfway through "They Don't Make 'em Like My Daddy Anymore," I was seized by a sudden inexplicable grief, and fled from the gym in tears.

My own dad was still alive then. He would, in fact, live for another twenty-three years. But that night on a hillside in Hazard, enveloped in Loretta's sweet sad song, the very thought of losing my father was more than I could bear.

He was born in 1918. They named him Arnold. A few days later when news came that a cousin had been killed in the war, they changed the baby's name to his – Luther Charles. He was the third child of David and Pearl Cornett Gabbard. There would be six more.

He grew up in Jackson County, at Letterbox, Mt. Zion, Gray Hawk and McKee. He played basketball at Tyner High School. All his life he loved shooting marbles, pitching horseshoes, playing croquet, and he was good at those things. Like a lot of other Kentuckians, he believed in the Democratic Party, the UK Wildcats, the Southern Baptist Convention, the family, and a good garden.

220

One of his grandfathers, Elijah Cornett, had been a Baptist preacher. Dad had grown up in the church, and he brought us up in the church, too. We were one of those every-time-the-door-opened kind of families, there for Sunday School, Sunday morning worship, Training Union, Sunday night service, Wednesday night prayer meeting, choir practice, Sunbeams, G.A.'s, business meetings and revivals.

Though deeply religious, my dad didn't judge other people or try to tell them how they ought to believe. And he never thought he had all the answers. After he died, I brought his Bibles home, a stack of them, well worn, with passages underlined and notes penciled in the margins.

Dad's Bibles open naturally to the parables of Jesus, the ones about the harvest, the vineyard, the sower and the seed. Once he preached the sermon at church. His topic was stewardship of the soil.

He majored in agriculture at Berea College, working his way through as a janitor in the music building. I like to think about him as a young man, mopping the wooden floor in the long dark hall while, from the practice rooms, the air filled with Mozart, Verdi and Chopin.

He was in a medical unit in Africa and Italy during World War II. He didn't talk about it much, but once he told me that it was a lot like the TV show *M*A*S*H*, except it wasn't funny.

After the war he taught vocational agriculture at McKee High School, and later worked for the USDA Soil Conservation Service. And he grew gardens. Not ordinary gardens, either, but the most beautiful vegetables, the sweetest melons, the biggest strawberries. He labored over his plants, hoeing morning and evening, sweating till his shirt was soaked. I never heard him complain about it.

He had broad shoulders, brown hair, and clear blue eyes that could widen suddenly with surprise. After so many summers in the sun, his arms and face turned so brown they stayed that way even through the winter. He smelled of after shave, pipe tobacco, and apples.

And he was gentle, his hugs and pats on the shoulder as soft and sweet as a child's. I saw him fret with worry many times, but I never heard him swear, not once, and he never raised his voice. He didn't have that in him. He'd taken to heart those early Bible lessons about meekness and humility.

Although he was the first in his family to go to college, and the only one to finish, and although he was successful in his profession, he never considered himself very smart. But he was. And he was funny, too. In any crowd, he was the one who made everybody laugh. He had this quirky sense of humor, and he kept it, almost to the end.

After he got sick, it was hard for him to stand up long enough to take a shower, but one day he tried. When he got out, his feet and legs were so swollen he was having trouble getting his house slippers on.

"Are you sure these are your shoes?" I asked him.

"They're my shoes," he said, "but I don't think these are my feet."

Dad was generous, but he didn't like to waste money, and he wanted to be sure he had plenty of blackberries in the freezer. A neighbor asked for a bag one time and ended up taking a pillowcase full. When Dad protested, I reminded him that the Bible says, if somebody asks you for your coat, give him your cloak also.

"It doesn't say anything about blackberries," he told me.

He was lying in the hospital bed with a broken hip, hooked up to an IV and oxygen. The preacher had come to see him and was about to leave. "Well, Luther, be good," Brother Terry said.

"Physically, preacher, I will be without sin," Dad replied.

He died three years ago. I still miss him so much that it is sometimes hard to breathe.

And it's been hard to go through his things, his slingshots and marbles, his Rook decks and seed catalogs, the candy he hid away, the wallet with the picture of me in fourth grade, the miscellaneous and often unidentifiable flea market items, every birthday and Father's Day card I ever gave him.

I don't know why I ran out of the gym that night at Hazard, what I thought I was running from, or where I thought I could go to get away from it. Perhaps it was a kind of premonition of the grief that was to come.

Or maybe I just knew, even then, that Loretta had it right. They don't make 'em like my daddy anymore.

6/20/02

∽

House for Sale

"S*pacious older home,* solid construction. On three acres within city limits of London, Kentucky. Convenient to shopping, restaurants, medical facilities. Garden plots, three outbuildings, small orchard. Quiet street, backs up to woods. Garage, full basement, plenty of storage. Central gas and air. Fireplaces, porches and deck. Gently sloping lawn, scenic views. Same owners for forty years."

∽

We moved there in 1963, when the house was still new. The red brick and Bedford stone, the big picture windows and gleaming hardwood floors seemed quite modern to us then. This was my parents' dream house, the one they'd been looking for, the one they'd been saving for out of Mother's salary as a schoolteacher and Dad's as a county soil conservationist.

In 1963 the house was well outside the city limits, in a part of town where, in the decades since, stores, restaurants and office buildings have replaced farm fields and pastures. But on a clear day, past the new shopping centers and the traffic on the bypass, you can still see layers of mountain ridges along the horizon. Their soft undulating lines and changing colors reminded us that the hills we'd come from, further east and south, were not so far away.

The house sits on a three-acre parcel of land which, the appraiser tells us, as if he is breaking bad news, "does not lend itself to commercial development." It has, however, lent itself well over the years to the development of marigolds, zinnias and evening primroses, to the growth of Kentucky Wonder beans and Early Girl tomatoes, to the commerce of pollinating bees and the bustling of wrens.

There was room enough for being together, for watching Kentucky basketball, for Sunday and holiday feasts, for family singing and stories.

And there was room to be alone. Dad "piddled," he called it, in his basement workshop. Mother claimed spaces for quilting, drying flowers and painting pictures. In her own room, my sister listened to records and practiced the clarinet. I locked my door to read novels and think about boys.

After our parents died, my sister and I began to realize how much storage space there is in that house. Raised in Eastern Kentucky during the Depression, Mother and Dad didn't believe in wasting anything, or even in throwing much away. We've sorted through a small mountain of objects they left us – everything from stone marbles to college textbooks from the 1940s to the world's largest collection of Kool-Whip containers and miscellaneous plastic lids. Sorting through it all, we've sorted through our own pasts and our parents' pasts, through our lives together in that now-empty house with the For Sale sign out front.

"Shown by appointment. Call Debbie at Sally Davidson Realty, 877-3000." All property rights accrue to buyer. Memories retained by seller.

6/3/03

Fare Ye Well, Old Joe Clark

***N**ext time you're on Highway 11* between Oneida and Booneville, take KY 577 up Sextons Creek. Just past the junction of 577 and 1350, you'll come to a roadside historical marker. Kentucky Historical Society Marker #1382 commemorates the man who may be the most famous Eastern Kentuckian of all time – Old Joe Clark.

I went down to Old Joe Clark's. He was eatin' supper.
Stubbed my toe on a table leg, stuck my nose in the butter.

The marker explains that Joe Clark, who was born in Clay County September 18, 1839, and lived all his life on Sextons Creek, was the inspiration for the well-known and many-versed folk song, "Old Joe Clark." (Not to be confused with the banjo player and country comedian who later called himself "Old Joe Clark" after the famous song.)

Old Joe Clark built a house, eighteen stories high.
Every story in that house was filled with chicken pie.

Probably the melody came first, without words, as a traditional frontier fiddle tune, still popular today among old-time fiddlers and Bluegrass banjo pickers.

Then, the story goes, some of Old Joe's friends began making up verses for the song, which has spread throughout the United States and the world, picking up more verses along the way.

Old Joe Clark, the preacher's son, preached all o'er the plain.
The only text he ever knew was High, Low, Jack & the Game.

The roadside marker calls Old Joe Clark "a shiftless and rough mountaineer of that day," which sounds like a bit of an insult, not just to Old Joe, but to us and our ancestors as well.

Joe Clark may have been something of a womanizer, but he doesn't appear to have been all that shiftless. He farmed, kept store, bought and sold property, grew orchards, and manufactured and sold moonshine back when it was legal to do so.

Old Joe Clark's a good old man, I'll tell you the reason why.
He keeps good liquor 'round his house: good old Rock & Rye.

Clark volunteered with the Union Army when the Civil War broke out, but became ill and was discharged.

I went down to Old Joe Clark's. He was sick in bed.
I run my finger down his throat, pulled out a chicken's head.

And Old Joe Clark was never really old. He was murdered in 1885 or '86, when he was still in his forties. One version of the story says that he was killed by a Howard in a scheme to get hold of some of Joe's property. After shooting Joe Clark, Howard fled to Beattyville, where, on a bridge a few days later, he himself was stabbed to death by two men from Clay County.

Old Joe Clark is dead and gone. I hope he's gone to rest.
Of all the gals he used to love, he loved my gal the best.

Fare ye well, Old Joe Clark. Good-bye, Betty Brown.
Fare ye well, Old Joe Clark. Fare ye well, I'm gone.

9/18/03

Afterword

***I** have a patchwork* flannel quilted skirt that my momma and sister made for me one Christmas. When I need comfort or feel really good about where I'm from, I put on that skirt. My sister calls me the Appalachian Queen whenever she sees me in it and that's how I feel, like a queen, secure in my place, knowing where I'm from and completely sure of my purpose. When I wear that skirt, I am home, home is good and where I want to be. For me, working on any project with Anne Shelby is like wearing that skirt.

So, when she asked if I'd take some photos of her for this book, I was tickled to death (one of them is on this page). Anne met me in the driveway with a tobacco stick, a passel of barking dogs and an outstretched arm. She asked me if I had any ideas on how we could let people know what she was trying to convey with the title. I told her it made me laugh my head off. That's what we had to go on.

We put all our ideas together and what you see on the cover is what we came up with. Despite all our effort, I guess you'll take it however you want.

– JAMIE JOHNSON
East Bernstadt, Kentucky
February 2006